*I am delighted to recommend
this booklet and the entire
RZIM Critical Questions Series
to you. Written in a popular style and
engaging manner, these booklets are
authored by many notable thinkers and
respected scholars.*

*They are uniquely and specifically
designed for those who have
questions about—and even
difficulties with—belief in God and the
credibility of the Christian faith.*

*Christian believers, too, will greatly
benefit from this series, which will serve
as an important tool to present and
defend their faith in the
marketplace of ideas.*

*I am convinced that these
remarkable booklets will not
disappoint in their readability and in
their persuasiveness for those honestly
seeking answers to life's deepest questions
and to the cultural
confusion around us.*

Ravi K. Zacharias

WHY ISN'T GOD MORE OBVIOUS?

Finding the God Who Hides and Seeks

Paul K. Moser

has a Ph.D. in philosophy from Vanderbilt University and is Professor and Chairperson of Philosophy at Loyola University of Chicago. His authored books include *Philosophy After Objectivity* (Oxford University Press) and *Knowledge and Evidence* (Cambridge University Press). He is co-author of *The Theory of Knowledge* (Oxford University Press). His edited works include *A Priori Knowledge* (Oxford University Press), *Rationality in Action* (Cambridge University Press), and *Empirical Knowledge* (Rowman & Littlefield). He is also co-editor of *Human Knowledge* (Oxford University Press), *Moral Relativism* (Oxford University Press), and *The Hiddenness of God* (forthcoming, Cambridge University Press). His articles have appeared in such journals as *Philosophy of Science*, *American Philosophical Quarterly*, *The Philosophical Quarterly*, *Noûs*, *History of Philosophy Quarterly*, and *Christian Scholar's Review*. He is General Editor of three book series, including Oxford Handbooks of Philosophy and Routledge Contemporary Introductions to Philosophy. He lives with his wife and two daughters in Wilmette, Illinois.

ISBN 1-930107-16-1

WHY ISN'T GOD MORE OBVIOUS?

Finding the God Who Hides and Seeks

Paul K. Moser

"...people say to me continually, 'Where is your God?'" (Psalm 42:3, NRSV)

"When you search for me, you will find me; if you seek me with all your heart, I will let you find me, says the Lord...." (Jeremiah 29:13-14, NRSV)

WOULD AN ALL-LOVING GOD HIDE?

♆ Chapter 1 ♆

Somebody once asked atheist Bertrand Russell what he would say if after death he met God. Russell's reply: "God, you gave us insufficient evidence." This reply captures an attitude of many people, including theists as well as atheists and agnostics. Why isn't God more obvious? If God exists, why doesn't God give us "sufficient evidence" of God's existence? We shall see that God does indeed supply sufficient decisive evidence. The decisive evidence supplied is, however, profoundly different from what we naturally expect.

Let's use the term "God" as a supreme title. It requires of any possible holder: (a) worthiness of worship and full life-commitment and thus (b) moral perfection and (c) an all-loving character. Lacking a better candidate for title-holder, let's consider the God of Abraham, Isaac, Jacob, and Jesus. We thus shall speak of "the Hebraic God," and correspondingly of "Hebraic theism" as the view that the Hebraic God actually exists. Is Hebraic theism true? Does our available evidence indicate, as Russell held, that Hebraic theism is false or at least unreasonable? Can we reasonably trust a God whom we neither see nor control?

We sometimes have misguided expectations regarding God. So our expected indicators of God's existence may mislead us. Correct indicators of God's existence will line up with God's character and plans. So we should ask what *God* may be like and plan to do, before we settle on *our* expectations for God. Perhaps, however, we are unable to understand or to know God on our own and thus must learn *from God*. The apostle Paul held that "it is part of the wisdom of God that the world did not know God through its own wisdom" (1 Corinthians 1:21). We do not need to assume now that Paul is right. We should, however, be open to the *possible* truth of Paul's view. In that spirit, we shall note a number of scriptural passages. Let's treat them as suggestions of how we *might* think of God and God's ways. If they ultimately make the best available sense of our human situation, they will merit our serious consideration as indicators of reality. The scriptures noted will give specific content to our talk of the Hebraic God. In ignoring the scriptures, we easily fall prey to abstract, speculative, or wishful thinking about God and thereby miss the explanatory profundity of Hebraic theism.

The Hebraic God is famous for hiding at times. The theme of divine hiding reverberates throughout the Hebrew scriptures and the New Testament. So we are left with an all-loving God who sometimes hides from people. Many people assume that an all-loving God's existence, if real, would be obvious to all normal humans. God's existence is not, however, *obvious* to all normal humans. So, according to many people, we may reasonably deny that God actually exists. How could an all-loving God fail to manifest God's reality in a way that removes all doubt about God's existence? Some normal humans do not believe that God exists. They claim *not* to have adequate evidence for reasonable belief that God exists. Would an all-loving God permit this? How could this be, if God is indeed all-loving?

Divine hiding bears on theists as well as atheists and agnostics. Psalm 10 complains about God's hiding. "Why, O Lord, do you stand far off? Why do you hide yourself in times of trouble?" (Psalm 10:1, NRSV; cf. Job 13:24). Psalm 30 laments God's hiding after times of the psalmist's confident security. "When I felt secure, I said, 'I will never be shaken.' O Lord, when you favored me, you made my mountain stand firm; but when you hid your face, I was dismayed" (Psalm 30:7, NIV; cf. Psalm 104:27-29). Psalm 44 expresses outright annoyance at God's hiding, suggesting that God's hiding is actually morally negligent. "Rouse yourself! Why do you sleep, O Lord? Awake, do not cast us off forever! Why do you hide your face? Why do you forget our affliction and oppression?" (Psalm 44:23-24, NRSV). The subject of God's hiding is no intellectual parlor-game in the Psalms. It cuts to the core of the psalmists' understanding of God and at times prompts lament from God's people.

Isaiah 45:15 sums up a central Hebraic view of God: "Truly you are a God who hides himself, O God of Israel, the Savior." The claim is *not* that God hides always or that we have no evidence of God's reality. The suggestion is that divine hiding occurs at times for God's own purposes. God's purposes in hiding may be unclear and even impenetrable to us at times. This does not mean, however, that they are unclear in every situation.

God's hiding is sometimes a response to human disobedience and moral indifference toward God (Deuteronomy 31:16-19, 32:19-20; Psalm 89:46; Isaiah 59:2; Micah 3:4). We should not, however, jump to a simplistic account of divine hiding. God hides at times for *various* purposes in relating to humans. Divine hiding is *not* always a judgment on human disobedience or indifference. It is often a constructive effort to encourage deeper human focus, longing, and gratitude toward God. God thus aims to take us, even if painfully, to our own deepest resources and their inadequacy, where "deep calls to deep" (Psalm 42:7; cf. Psalm 130:1). In apprehending God's *absence*, we can achieve a deeper, more profound appreciation of God's presence. God's absence can indeed make one's heart grow fonder of God, at least in some cases. By sharpening the contrast between God's *presence* and *absence*, God can highlight the surpassing value of God's presence.

Divine hiding, like everything else God does, seeks to advance God's good kingdom by promoting what is good for all concerned. So we must keep divine hiding in the context of God's main desire to have people lovingly know God and thereby to become loving as God is loving. As Isaiah 65:2 reports, "I [God] held out my hands all day long to a rebellious people, who walk in a way that is not good" (cf. Romans 10:21). God's holding out hands toward people stems from the same concern as Jesus' weeping over Jerusalem (Luke 19:41; cf. 13:34). God desires that people turn, for their own good, to the loving God in filial communion and faithful obedience. God's *primary* aim is not to hide but rather to include all people in God's *family* as beloved children under God's fatherly guidance. A loving filial relationship with God is God's main goal for every human. This means that God wants us to *love*, to *treasure*, God as our Father, not just to believe that God exists (Deuteronomy 6:5; Mark 12:30; James 2:19). So production of mere reasonable belief that God exists will not meet God's higher aim for us. For our own good, God is after something more profound and more transforming than simple reasonable belief about God. Mere reasonable belief is no match for personal transformation toward God's loving character.

Divine hiding typically results from a human deficiency. An arguable exception comes from Jesus' cry of abandonment on the cross: "My God, my God, why have you forsaken me?" (Mark 15:34). Jesus felt forsaken by his Father at that time. Perhaps Jesus learned a deeper level of obedience toward his Father from this excruciating case of divine hiding (cf. Hebrews 5:8). Even so, according to a common biblical theme, God takes no pleasure in staying away from humans or being rejected by them (Ezekiel 18:23,32; 33:11; 2 Peter 3:9; 1 Timothy 2:3-4). As all-loving, God seeks friendship with all humans under God's fatherly love (James 2:23; John 3:16-17, 15:14-15). We distort God's loving character whenever we portray God otherwise.

The epistle of James puts decisive responsibility on us humans: "Come near to God and God will come near to you" (4:8; cf. Jeremiah 29:13; Malachi 3:7). According to various biblical writers, we should take stock of our standing before God if God is hiding from us. We then may need to change something in our lives, perhaps certain attitudes and practices against the ways of God. For important lists of attitudes and practices against and in favor of God's ways, see Mark 7:21-22; Galatians 5:19-26. These lists give specificity to the kind of unselfish love characteristic of God. Friendship with God, like genuine human friendship, depends on unselfish love.

In the case of "blameless and upright" Job, a presumptuous attitude about knowledge of God needed revision (Job, chapters 38-42). Similarly, many people today presume to know how a loving God *should* or *must* intervene in our world, if God is to be loving. For example, many people suggest that an all-loving God would have to keep the world free of evil. What, however, determines how God *should* be revealed? What standard of clarity must God's self-revelation meet? A loving God would not, and should not, be bound by superficial human expectations. Human expectations must be transformed, for the good of humans, toward the profoundly loving character of God. This disturbing and humbling lesson is central to Hebraic theism. It reminds us that our "wisdom" may not add up to God's wisdom (Isaiah 29:14; 1 Corinthians 1:19-20). Our expectations may be shallow or even mistaken in comparison with God's loving character and intentions. Due humility is thus appropriate in approaching the Hebraic God.

HIDING AND AUTHORITY IN JESUS

The New Testament characterizes God as hiding either himself or important information about God from certain people. Jesus prays as follows regarding the lessons of his mission.

> I thank you, Father, Lord of heaven and earth, because you have hidden these things

from the wise and the intelligent and have revealed them to infants; yes, Father, for such was your gracious will. All things have been handed over to me by my Father; and no one knows the Son except the Father, and no one knows the Father except the Son and anyone to whom the Son chooses to reveal him (Matthew 11:25-26, NRSV; cf. Luke 10:21-22).

Jesus claims that he is the unique son and sole revealer of God and thus has unequaled authority among humans. Such a claim would seem delusional at best on the lips of any human other than Jesus. Let's observe some of the indications of Jesus' authority. Jesus himself, as a personal image of God, may serve as a special kind of evidence of God's reality.

The life of Jesus exhibited, in word and deed, a kind of authority and power unique among humans. So a central message of the New Testament is that Jesus has unsurpassed authority and power in human history. Jesus remarks that acceptance (or rejection) of him amounts to acceptance (or rejection) of God (Matthew 10:40). In addition, Jesus claims authority to forgive sins apart from God's Temple (Mark 2:1-12) and to arrange for the final judgment as God's king (Luke 22:29-30). Likewise, Jesus symbolically presents himself as the long-awaited everlasting king of Israel, after Zechariah 9:9, in his humble entry into Jerusalem on a colt (Mark 11:1-10). He also intimates that he is King David's Lord (Mark 12:35-37), and that he is greater than even King Solomon (Luke 11:31). Indeed, in reply to a question from John the Baptist (Luke 7:18-23), he alludes to Isaiah 61:1-2 and 35:5-6 to suggest that he is God's Messiah. Similarly, Jesus claims to be the messianic son of God in response to the chief priests (Mark 14:61-64). This claim, according to Mark 14:64, elicits the charge that Jesus is guilty of blasphemy, of exalting himself in a way that dishonors God.

In his own ministry, Jesus suggested, the kingdom of God has arrived. "If it is by the finger of God that I cast out the demons, then the kingdom of God has come to you" (Luke 11:20, NRSV). In the parable of the vine-yard (Mark 12:1-12) Jesus suggests that he is God's rejected (beloved) son who is heir to the things of God. In keeping with this theme, Jesus functions as the one uniquely qualified to send the Spirit of God to empower people (Mark 1:8; Acts 2:32-33). In addition, Jesus claims that his death will inaugurate the (new) covenant for many people (Mark 14:24). He thus suggests that his death has saving (or, redemptive) significance for others. Some Jewish literature around the turn of the eras acknowledges that human suffering can atone for sin, even for the sins of others (cf. 4 Maccabees 6:27-30, 9:23-25). The novelty is that Jesus—this Galilean outcast—regarded his death as the means of God's new *covenant* of redemption. The covenant is God's loving plan to save humans from their destructive ways.

New Testament scholar E.P. Sanders observes that Jesus himself shared the Gospel writers' view that "he fulfilled the hopes of the prophets." He adds that "Jesus' actual claim may have been... not only spokesman for, but viceroy of, God; and not just in a political kingdom but in the kingdom of God."[1] The previous New Testament data suggest that Jesus regarded himself as God's unique Priest, Judge, King, Messiah, Son, and Redeemer (=Savior). He saw himself as the one sent by God to fulfill the hopes of Israel for an everlasting kingdom under God. No other human could make such authoritative claims with any real plausibility. Jesus thus shatters the limits of human authority in a way that merits our attention. Jesus is no mere moral reformer, spiritual guru, or philosophical sage. He is either (i) patently insane (Mark 3:21), (ii) Satanic (Mark 3:22), or (iii) God's unique son and viceroy. Sanders himself rightly concludes: "He was not a madman."[2] His not being Satanic should go without saying, after one attends to the pattern of his life and teaching. The third of our three options thus recommends itself seriously for our endorsement. So we should take Jesus' claim about divine hiding seriously.

WHAT KIND OF KNOWING SUITS GOD?

🎵 Chapter 2 🎵

In his prayer of Matthew 11:25-26, Jesus speaks of knowing "the Son" and "the Father." He is speaking of a kind of knowledge that differs from mere justified true belief that God exists. Jesus is speaking of knowing God *as authoritative and giving Father*. Perhaps you know that God exists as First Cause, Intelligent Designer, or Ground of Being. Knowing God *as Lord, or Master*, who is your righteously gracious Father is, however, significantly different. Devoted to the latter kind of knowing, Jesus addressed God as "Abba" (best translated as "Father"). The Greek New Testament's retention of this Aramaic term (Mark 14:36; Galatians 4:5; Romans 8:15) offers warrant for treating "Abba" as part of the customary vocabulary of Jesus. Jesus' customary use of "Abba" to address God distinguished him significantly from his contemporaries. God is, however, portrayed as the Father of God's people in the Hebrew scriptures (for example, Psalms 89:26, 103:13; Isaiah 63:16).

FILIAL KNOWLEDGE OF GOD

Proper knowledge of God, according to Jesus, requires your standing in a humble, faithful, and loving child-parent, or *filial*, relationship to God as your righteously gracious Father. Unfortunately, such *filial knowledge* rarely surfaces in philosophy of religion or even in Christian approaches to knowledge of God. New Testament scholar James Dunn observes that Jesus' awareness of being God's beloved son was an "existential conviction," and not a matter of merely intellectual assent. "He *experienced* a relation of sonship — felt such an intimacy with God, such an

10

approval by God, dependence on God, responsibility to God, that the only words adequate to express it were 'Father' and 'son'.[3] Jesus' experience of being God's son is clearly expressed in his prayers (for example, Mark 14:36; Luke 10:21-22; Matthew 26:42). Indeed, Jesus seems to have regarded filial prayer toward God as an ideal avenue to proper, filial knowledge of God and to God's saving power (Mark 9:29). Such prayer is primarily a matter of asking what God wants from us rather than what we want from God. *God* rightly leads God's family. We do not. Humans properly submit to God for guidance and knowledge of God. We must let God be God.

We come to know other human persons by actively relating to them in personal interaction with them. Likewise, we come to know God via personal interaction whereby we become personally accountable to God. You could not responsibly apprehend the reality of your parents' love for you apart from a sincere personal relationship with them. An analogous point holds for your responsibly apprehending the reality of God's love. So filial knowledge of God is not just knowledge that another object in the universe exists. The Hebraic conception of filial knowledge of God requires that one know God not as a mere *object* but as the supreme *subject* who is Lord of all, including one's own life. Such knowledge requires the responsiveness of a filial personal relationship with God. It calls for a proper family relationship with God as the proper loving head of the family. We must *enter into*, *commit to*, and *participate in*, a loving relationship with God. This is no mere intellectual matter. Likewise, your entering into a friendship or a marriage relationship exceeds thinking and reasoning.

New Testament scholar C.H. Dodd has helpfully contrasted Greek and Hebraic conceptions of knowledge.

> ... for the Greek, to know God means to contemplate the ultimate reality in its changeless essence. For the Hebrew, to know God is to acknowledge Him in His

works and to respond to His claims. While for the Greek knowledge of God is the most highly abstract form of pure contemplation, for the Hebrew it is essentially ... to experience His dealings with men in time, and to hear and obey His commands.[4]

Elucidating the relevant Hebrew term for knowledge, *yada*, G. J. Botterweck reports: "'To know Yahweh [the covenant God of Israel]' refers to a practical, religio-ethical relationship."[5] Likewise, Old Testament scholar Bernhard Anderson characterizes Hebraic knowledge of God as "the kind of personal relationship with God that is manifest in social responsibility."[6] Being inherently *personal*, God properly reveals himself *personally*, not merely as an impersonal power, sign, argument, or proof. The Old Testament book of Hosea depicts proper knowledge of God in terms of a loyal marriage relationship (Hosea 2:16-20; cf. Isaiah 54:6). Such knowledge of God results from God's gracious self-revelation, not from typical human ways that are self-crediting or exclusive. For our own good, we cannot know God on our own self-serving terms. We rather must be amenable to God's better terms for knowing God, and this requires genuine humility on our part.

In the prayer of Matthew 11:25-27, Jesus thanks his Father for hiding his ways from people unwilling to enter a humble filial relationship with God. He thus assumes that it is good for God to maintain God's unmatched value rather than to neglect, or otherwise to compromise, the value of a humble filial relationship with God. In a similar vein, Jesus suggests that the kingdom of God is "like treasure hidden in a field" (Matthew 13:44; cf. Luke 19:42). God's valuable ways may require some human searching (Jeremiah 29:13-14; Matthew 7:7), as such searching can highlight their unsurpassed value for us. It can also show that we are unable to find God on our own, thereby prompting some humility in us. The Hebraic God wants humans to be fully engaged with God, even via our lament and protest in the face of God's hiding, as the Psalms illustrate. Such engagement will save us from fatal apathy toward God. God's occasional hiding thus does not entail that God is resistant, grudging, or deceptive toward humans (cf. Luke 12:32; Isaiah 65:1-2). It aims for our valuing, our treasuring, God above all else. Likewise, a loving earthly father will conduct himself in ways that maintain his value as father of his family.

Divine hiding stems from God's upholding the value of God's invaluable loving ways. God sustains the value of God's ways of human renewal in the presence of people who would compromise this value to their own detriment. For instance, we would readily sidestep God's challenges to our selfishness if we could. Having preeminent value, God's loving ways must remain sacred and not be diminished in value (cf. Matthew 7:6). We must treasure God and God's ways. God's primary goal in self-revelation is transformation of recipients toward God's loving character. This goal will not be satisfied by a revelation resulting just in one's reasonably believing that God exists. A person can reasonably believe that God exists but hate God. So God must be careful, and at times subtle, to have God's loving self-manifestation elicit a freely given response of humble love rather than fear, indifference, arrogance, or hate. Likewise, our eliciting a response of love from children demands carefulness and subtlety on our part. God cares mainly about what and how we *love*, not just what we believe. God aims that we treasure God; for where our treasure is, there our heart is.

Proper moral education toward sacrificial love and reconciliation always has been difficult noncoercive business. Typically its important lessons must be *shown* to us in action rather than simply *stated* to us in sentences or arguments. We must learn such lessons by *living* them rather than merely thinking them. This holds true even when the moral educator is God. Accordingly the life and death of Jesus offer a noncoercive demonstration of God's self-giving love and a life-pattern of obedient love for humans.[7] Given the important reality of human free will (a requirement for genuine love), such moral education has no guarantee of success. Even when God is the loving educator, failure can result. For example, we can choose life-styles that sidestep our learning unselfish love. Not even God can enforce genuine reconciliation between humans and God, the heart of redemption, or salvation.

Consider some (transliterated) non-English language. *Abba yithqaddash shemakh. Tethe malkuthakh. Lakhman delimkhar, habh lan yoma dhen.* [= Father, hallowed be your name. Your kingdom come. Our bread for tomorrow, give us today.] Perhaps you did not initially apprehend the meaning of this Palestinian Jewish Aramaic. You may not even have been confident initially that this token actually has meaning. Perhaps you had at most a vague glimpse of some of its meaning. The problem lies not in the Aramaic token. It lies rather in the overall perspective of beliefs and other attitudes you bring to this token. Call this perspective your *receptive attitude*. The problem lies in your lack of appropriate exposure and sensitivity to Palestinian Jewish Aramaic. Perhaps your life has avoided the Aramaic vocabulary and grammar needed to grasp the previous token. So the reception of significant evidence sometimes depends on the receptive attitude of people.

Failure to receive some evidence stems from shortcomings in intended *recipients* of evidence. The evidence itself could still be flawless. An analogy arises. People whose receptive attitude is closed to God's "language" (or, program) of liberating love may be blinded from apprehending available evidence for the reality of God. The evidence may be readily available, just as our Aramaic token is meaningful. According to Jesus, however, we need appropriate "ears to hear and eyes to see" the available evidence (Mark 4:9). We need an attitudinal change by becoming genuinely receptive to God, in order to apprehend the available evidence in the right way. We need to turn, to repent, and thereby to become sincerely open to God. We must thereby renounce all obstacles to God, in order to make God our priority. God is, after all, second to none in importance.

14

We must acknowledge that on our own we humans have failed dismally at the program of all-inclusive redemption (or, salvation), including self-redemption. This failure occurs relative to serious challenges to our very existence (for example, death), to our well-being (for example, physical and mental decline), and to our moral standing (for example, our regrettable tendency to selfishness). Call these challenges our *human predicament*. We have no self-made or even self-discovered solution to our common human predicament of serious deficiencies. Only a personal caring God can rescue us from this undeniable predicament. This humbling acknowledgment is significant relative to our knowing God, as Jesus suggests in his prayer of Matthew 11:25. It requires that we change how we think of ourselves and of our relation to a righteously gracious God. It calls for our beginning and continuing a humble *filial* relationship after the pattern of Jesus, the unique son of God. It also recommends a change in our intentions regarding our conduct and habits. Such change is *volitional*, a matter of the will. It is not merely intellectual. Contrary to Plato, we can know what is right but fail to do or even to favor what is right. We need to have our *will* captured and transformed by God's love.

Our humble awareness of our needing God will displace us from the prideful center of self-importance in our supposed universe. This is illustrated by human behavior typical of confrontation with the Hebraic God. Such behavior includes one's bowing, falling, or covering oneself before God or God's heavenly representatives. See the cases of Moses (Exodus 3:6, 34:8), Elijah (1 Kings 19:13), Ezekiel (Ezekiel 1:28), Daniel (Daniel 10:5-9), Saul (Acts 9:4-9), and John (Revelation 1:13-18). We must become humble enough to receive God's gracious love as a *gift* rather than as an *earning*. Our pride interferes by laying claim to our *earning* God's love and thus robbing it of its status as amazing grace, or gift. (On the key role of humility before God in Hebraic theism, see Isaiah 57:15, 66:2; Psalms 34:18, 51:7.) Via transformation toward humility before God, we become able to appreciate the explanatory depth of Hebraic theism regarding the human predicament and condition. Our eyes and ears are thereby opened in new ways. Transformation of our will can thus contribute to our appreciation of Hebraic theism and its explanatory value. It can yield a new illuminating perspective on our common human predicament. Likewise, commitment to redirect focus can bring a new perspective on an ambiguous perceptual figure, such as the famous duck-rabbit figure:

In *Pensées*, the seventeenth-century philosopher Blaise Pascal emphasized the bearing of God's hiding on volitional transformation.

> God wishes to move the will rather than the mind. Perfect clarity would help the mind and harm the will. Humble their pride. (§234)

> If there were no obscurity man would not feel his corruption; if there were no light man could not hope for a cure. Thus it is not only right but useful for us that God should be partly concealed and partly revealed, since it is equally dangerous for man to know God without knowing his own wretchedness as to know his wretchedness without knowing God. (§446)[8]

Pascal's remarks illuminate some cases of divine hiding, even if other cases of hiding call for a more complex diagnosis. The evidence of God available to us fits well with the Hebraic view of God's *various* intentions in self-hiding and self-revealing. Whenever pertinent, God aims to displace false claimants to

16

God's throne. For our own good, God works against *idolatry* (commitment to false gods) and its destructive consequences. Sometimes divine hiding is an effective antidote to idolatry, but not always. Sometimes we settle for false gods instead of the true God. We do this whenever we persist in our selfishness. So our idolatrous habits run deep indeed.

Without suitable transformation, we may be blinded from recognizing God, owing to our own counterfeit "intelligence" and "wisdom" (1 Corinthians 1:19-25). We may then lack the kind of sincere openness, humility, and filial obedience appropriate to relating to the true God. We may then have assigned the authority of God to ourselves or to some other part of creation. In that case, we would be guilty of idolatry. We often promote *cognitive idolatry* by demanding a kind of knowledge of God inappropriate to a filial relationship with God.[9] For instance, we often want *controllable* knowledge of God analogous to our knowledge of household objects. In thus violating God's program of gracious salvation through transformation, we are slaves to selfishness and need to be set free. The wisdom of philosophers, however sophisticated, offers no means of freeing us from selfish fear of losing what we value (such as our supposed control). This wisdom lacks the needed power to set us free, to transform us from the inside out toward God's ideal of all-inclusive love. Only the freeing power of God's gracious offer of filial relationship meets this need. A loving earthly father can remove some of his child's fears. Likewise, a loving God can dissolve the fears that prompt human selfishness.

The extent to which we know God depends on the extent to which we are gratefully willing to participate in God's loving program of salvation (Jeremiah 22:13-17; Micah 6:6-8). Our filial relationship with God deepens as it yields our participation in God's redemptive program. God's program then becomes *our* program. So it is now obvious why we humans have difficulty in knowing God. The difficulty stems from our resisting participation in God's redemptive program of reconciliation. So it is the height of arrogance for us humans to saunter up to the question whether God exists as if we were automatically in an appropriate moral and cognitive position to handle it reliably. Careful reflection on the purposes inherent to an all-loving God recommends an approach less cavalier than that typical of inquiring humans. We are, after all, inquiring about a very special kind of agent with distinctive purposes, not just a household object or laboratory specimen. We humans often proceed as if we had a hard time remembering this. Perhaps we cannot easily abide a gracious Being who evades our self-approving cognitive nets. Stubbornly, we insist on our own inferior terms for salvation. We thereby sidestep the genuine article and settle for counterfeits. So we miss out on the abundant life provided by filial knowledge of God.

God, we noted, is not after mere justified true belief that God exists. God cares how we handle evidence of God's existence. The concern is whether we become loving in handling such evidence, in agreement with God's character. So contrary to a typical human attitude, knowledge of God is not a spectator sport. It is rather part of a process of God's thorough make-over of a person. It is, from our human standpoint, an *active commitment* to a morally transforming personal relationship. We come to know God only as God becomes *our God*, the Lord of our lives. God will then differ from a mere object of our contemplation, speculation, amusement, or self-indulgence. God refuses, for our own good, to become a mere idol of our thought or entertainment.

Proper knowledge of the Hebraic God is inherently ethical and practical rather than simply reflective. Spectators complaining from the far bleachers may in fact remain out in the bleachers, by their own self-isolating choice. Knowing God requires one's apprehending a call to come in from the remote bleachers and gratefully join God's plan of gracious salvation. This plan is no mere intellectual puzzle for philosophers or theologians. God is more serious than our mental gymnastics, for our own good. We have, after all, *lives* to form and to live, not just thoughts to think or intellectual puzzles to solve. God's call, in keeping with the call of Abraham, Jeremiah, Jesus, and Paul, requires that we commit to using our whole lives for the advancement of God's kingdom of self-giving love. So proper knowledge of God extends to our deepest attitudes and convictions. God is free of our superficial ways.

KNOWING IN JOHN'S GOSPEL

John's Gospel highlights the importance of the human will in human knowledge. In John 7:3-4, Jesus faces a problem of hiding raised by his own brothers (who, according to John 7:5, did not believe in him). His brothers tell him that nobody works in hiding while seeking to be known openly. Their challenge is straightforward: "Manifest yourself to the world" (John 7:4; cf. John 10:24). Jesus replies that the world hates him because he testifies that its works are evil. He suggests that the world has the wrong *attitude* toward him. John then portrays Jesus as teaching in the temple that if anyone *wills* to do the will of God, that person will know whether Jesus' teaching is from God (7:17). Note the importance of one's *willing* to obey God, as in a humble filial relationship with God. It is fitting, then, that this part of John's Gospel culminates in a dispute over *filial* association with either God or the devil (John 8:39-47). (See also the relevant filial language of one's being "born" again/from above in John 3:1-12, in connection with seeing/entering the kingdom of God and knowing the things of God.) A human filial response to God presupposes that *God* graciously takes the initiative in trying to establish a filial relationship. *God* first calls us to humble reception of God's transforming love. God loves us before we love God.

John 12:35-40 continues the theme of hiding. After predicting his death, Jesus advises his listeners to walk while they have the light, unless the darkness overtake them (v. 35). He suggests that understanding the things of God requires trust in God (v. 36). Christian faith is not, however, an ungrounded

19

response to inadequate evidence for God. It is not a "leap of faith." It is a filial attitude of obediently entrusting oneself to a faithful God who reveals himself as a righteously gracious Father (cf. John 14:1). Jesus hides from the unbelieving crowd. John links the unbelief to the kind of judgment described in Isaiah 6:10. "He has blinded their eyes and hardened their heart, unless they should see with their eyes and perceive with their heart, and turn for me to heal them" (cf. Mark 4:11-12). John suggests that the crowd's unbelief in the face of Jesus' miraculous signs led to hardening and blindness in understanding. So one's handling of the available evidence concerning God has serious consequences for one's understanding other considerations about God. The signs of God must be handled with utter seriousness, as one's very life is at stake. Assessing evidence of God is no parlor game.

John 14:21 portrays a grand promise from Jesus. "The person having my commandments and keeping them, that is the one who loves me; the person loving me will be loved by my Father, and I will love that person and manifest myself to him" (John 14:21). This amazing promise is general, applying to *anyone* keeping the commandments of Jesus. Note the importance of obedience and love, key factors that go well beyond reasonable belief that God exists. The promise has crucial volitional conditions. The prophet Hosea, we noted, uses a loyal marriage relationship as a model for knowing God. On this model, mutual respect and love will obviously be central to a knowledge relationship. We could use a relation of friendship to make the same point, in keeping with John 15:13-15.

One of Jesus' disciples restates the challenge from Jesus' brothers in John 7:4, asking why he will not manifest himself to the world (John 14:22). The disciples' thinking is familiar: why hide from the world if you have miraculous powers? Jesus offers a reply that highlights again the importance of the volitional human attitudes of love and obedience in relation to God. "If a person loves me, that person will keep my word, and my Father will love him, and we will come to him and make our home with him" (14:23). Jesus' reply assumes that the world does not love the things of God. So God's self-manifestation would not have the filial effect of love desired by God. Such a manifestation would thus compromise the value of God's self-revelation. In another context, Jesus remarks that "an evil and adulterous generation seeks a sign" (Matthew 12:39, 16:4; cf. Mark 8:12; John 6:30). Entertaining signs and wonders are typically ineffective toward a filial relationship with God. They do not cut deeply enough into one's character to elicit sacrificial love toward God. (Chapter 3 below considers this topic.) Jesus portrays God as desiring not mere acknowledgment or intellectual affirmation, but an attitude of filial, loving obedience toward God. For our own good, God wants us to treasure God as our Lord, as our loving Master.

The first epistle of John develops the theme that proper knowledge of God depends on a filial attitude of loving obedience toward God.

> By this we know that we have come to know [God], if we keep his commandments.... Whoever keeps his [God's] word, truly in this person the love of God is perfected. By this we know that we are in him. The one who claims to remain in him ought himself to behave as he [Jesus] behaved (1 John 2:3,5). The one who loves ... knows God. The one who does not love does not know God, because God is love (1 John 4:7-8).

John regards a filial attitude of loving obedience toward God as required and adequate for properly knowing God. So our not loving will preclude our knowing God. Note the central role of the son Jesus in this passage. Jesus serves as the practical model for genuine filial knowledge of God. The Gospel of John (6:30-36) identifies Jesus as the effective "sign" — the filial evidence — for us from God. God seeks to reveal God's character of personal love. So God sends Jesus to manifest God's self-giving love. Jesus is a sign unavailable to people closed or indifferent to God's gracious offer of filial relationship. Filial knowledge of God exemplifies the distinctive kind of personal knowledge of God central to Hebraic theism. Filial love is built into the very core of knowing the God of love. Other proposed ways of knowing God are but cheap counterfeits. The prophet Hosea would say that they involve harlotry rather than a loyal marriage. Efforts to know God without loving friendship with God miss the true character of the God of all-inclusive love. God, we might say, is hidden only in God's supreme love. God's occasional hiding is God's love obscured, owing to some deficiency on our part. This obscuring seeks to uphold the supreme value of God's love while God tries to bring us all deeper into that love.

What about evidence of God from prophecies, miracles, the empty tomb of Jesus, the post-resurrection transformation of the apostles, design in nature, and the reality of moral conscience? Such evidence enhances reasonable Christian commitment. Still, it is not *decisive* for filial knowledge of God. A person can accept such evidence without properly knowing God at all in a filial manner. One can acknowledge such evidence but still fail altogether to love God or to be committed to obey God. *Accepting such evidence* is one thing; *loving God* is another. This difference yields a sharp contrast between dead faith and saving faith. Saving faith is renewing faith, toward God's loving character.

Jesus demands of his followers a whole-hearted loving commitment toward God as genuinely loving Father (Mark 8:34-38; Matthew 8:18-22, 10:37-39). Such whole-hearted commitment finds no adequate basis in the uncertainties of theoretical inference about history or nature. Its needed basis, we shall see, is in the morally transforming presence of God's righteous love through filial relationship. Such a relationship is made available and exemplified by the self-giving life and death of God's unique son Jesus. The historical evidence is indeed significant. The Hebraic God works tirelessly in the turbulence of human history. God even sends his unique son into the historical fray to exhibit God's sacrificial love. Still, such evidence is not suitably decisive for filial knowledge of God. Our filial knowledge of God must be liberating, reconciling, and morally transforming toward God's character. Historical evidence cannot fill that bill. By analogy, your having historical evidence about a loyal marriage falls short of your lovingly participating in a loyal marriage. Similarly, your knowing about a valuable friendship does not add up to your having a valuable friendship.

We must know God's transforming love directly in filial relationship, not just in historical evidence about God's love. C.H. Dodd has put this key lesson in context. "Perhaps one of the most striking features of the early Christian movement was the re-appearance of a confidence that [one] can know God immediately.... Jesus Christ, with a confidence that to the timid traditionalism of His time appeared blasphemous, asserted that He knew the Father and was prepared to let others into that knowledge. He did so ... by making others sharers in His own attitude to God."[10] Jesus' shareable "attitude" to God is inherently filial, as illustrated by the Lord's Prayer (Matthew 6:9-15) and the testing of Jesus in Gethsemane (Mark 14:32-36). Jesus directly experienced his Father's gracious self-giving love and obediently returned the same sacrificial love to his Father. We are called to do the same, even in the same whole-hearted manner.

Our discerning that Jesus himself offers a compelling reason to acknowledge God is no mere intellectual matter. We must be genuinely willing to exemplify the kind of God-centered excellence shown by Jesus in his relation to God as Father. We must be willing to appropriate Jesus' teaching that we humans have failed at being properly filial toward our righteously gracious Father. We must also be willing to acknowledge sincerely that this is the worst kind of personal failure possible. We thus must render judgment against ourselves, judgment that we have rebelled against our filial responsibility before God (cf. Luke 15:11-32). This is the beginning of what Jesus called *repentance* and demanded of his followers (Mark 1:15, 6:12; Luke 13:3,5). It is crucial to our appropriating God's forgiving love. Such repentance calls for humble recognition that we are not entitled on our own to know God as Father. We must recognize that filial knowledge of God can come only as a gracious gift, not as a prideful earning. Likewise, true love must be received, not bought or coerced. Accordingly we cannot buy or force even genuine earthly friendship.

The excellence of Jesus is ultimately *revealed* to people sincerely willing to honor such excellence with their lives, and not *just* their thoughts (Matthew 16:15-17). Divine grace aims to remove community-destroying pride about good works and status (Luke 15:28-32; 1 Corinthians 4:7; Ephesians 2:9). Likewise, God uses the gift of God's self-revelation to remove pride about self-crediting intellectual means of finding God (cf. 1 Corinthian 1:26-29). Argument can indeed remove some obstacles to God's self-revelation. God's *Spirit* is, however, the final source and seal of such revelation. God's Spirit makes the wisdom of God a liberating power absent from worldly wisdom. Proper knowledge of God thus has its ultimate source in the Spirit of God, who testifies about God immediately to our spirits (Romans 8:16; cf. 1 John 4:13, 5:6-9; 1 Corinthians 2:12-14). God's Spirit convicts us of our unloving ways and calls us to loving relationship with God and others, even our enemies.

In keeping with Jesus' prayer of Matthew 11:25-27, we ultimately know God by gracious revelation through God's Spirit. Christian theory of knowledge must therefore give a central role to the immediate testimony and power of God's revealing Spirit. Paul put the point clearly. "We have received not the spirit of the world but the Spirit from God, in order that we may know the things freely given to us by God" (1 Corinthians 2:12; cf. 4:7, 12:3; Romans 8:14-16; John 3:8; 1 John 5:20). So people will be unable to appreciate the cognitive and spiritual depths of Hebraic theism from outside, apart from filial reception of the Spirit of God. Jesus thus connects (a) our finding, and receiving from, God with (b) our receiving the Father's Holy Spirit (Luke 11:9-13). Our filial knowing of God thus depends on our receiving the Spirit of God. This does not call, however, for an irrational leap of faith. God faithfully supplies adequate, convicting grounds for our calling on the name of the Lord.

The Hebraic God is anything but cognitively "safe," or controllable. We cannot control either God or God's hiding on occasion. So we cannot remove God's hiding with our self-made recipes. The Hebraic God leaves us empty-handed when we insist on seeking with our self-made tools, including familiar recipe-like spiritualities. We therefore cannot "solve" the problem of divine hiding if a solution requires a self-made tool to remove such hiding. We are, after all, neither God nor God's advisers (Isaiah 40:13-14). At best we are God's loyal children. So we should not be surprised that we lack our own devices to banish God's occasional hiding. We have no warrant for trying to control God, just as children should not try to control their loving earthly father.

God's ways need not line up with our preferred ways for God. This is one central message of the biblical writings. It fits with God's distinctive role in the human predicament. God is the supreme Gift-Giver who seeks us prior to our seeking God. This is what Hebraic covenant love (*chesed*) and New Testament grace (*charis*) are all about. If we love God, it is because God *first* loved us, desired us, and offered God's love to us (1 John 4:10,19; Romans 5:8). The order here is crucial, cognitively and morally.[11] For our own good, God calls for our grateful surrender and obedience to the merciful Gift-Giver. Our anxiously casting about with our own self-crediting tools for finding God is thus misplaced (Romans 10:6-9). The Hebraic God is not to be found by our own self-promoting recipes.

We often prefer not to settle for grateful acceptance of God's gift of (a) personal filial knowledge of God and (b) God's personal assurance of God's presence. We often prefer to *earn* our knowledge of God on our own terms. We prefer to have cognitive control here as elsewhere in our lives. Such control offers us a desired basis for prideful boasting in ourselves. The Hebraic God, in contrast, favors a cognitive approach of humble, self-giving compassion, where God serves as the humble Gift-Giver of knowledge and we serve as grateful recipients. It is only out of our acknowledged weakness—our recognized need—that we have true humility and gratitude toward God. We should let God be God (and thus be transformingly gracious) even in our acquiring knowledge of God. Analogously, children should permit their earthly father to be gracious toward them. Otherwise, a loving relationship will be impossible.

Our habitual refusal to love sacrificially as God loves blinds us from seeing the things of God. As 1 John 4:3 states: "Whoever does not love does not know God, because God is love." Our recurring attitude of prideful ingratitude is particularly self-blinding with regard to God, just as it undermines earthly friendships. Such ingratitude is the poisonous root of resistance to God. It is a corrosive attitude that drives God into hiding. Via gratitude for gifts received, in contrast, we come to trust and even to love God, thereby growing in filial knowledge of God. Perhaps God would become less hidden to us if we spent more time gratefully talking and listening *to* God rather than merely talking about God. We must welcome the gift of God's presence for it to benefit us by transforming us. Proper reception of God demands inviting and welcoming God with gratitude. Mere reasoning, however sound, will not fill this bill. Reasoning is at best a delivery truck. God must supply the priceless treasure (God's love) to be delivered. Similarly, in earthly friendship we must receive the gift of friendship, thereby going beyond reasoning about friendship. Love always moves beyond mere reflection, to commitment and action.

Let's distinguish: (a) *propositional* knowledge that God exists, and (b) *filial* knowledge as one's standing in a humble, faithful, and loving relationship to God as righteously gracious Father. Filial knowledge of God *requires* propositional (or, intellectual) knowledge that God exists, but it *exceeds* propositional knowledge. One can know that God exists, as we noted, but fail to love God. Filial knowledge of God, in contrast, includes our being reconciled to God (at least to some degree) through a loving filial relationship with God. It requires our entrusting ourselves as children to God in grateful love. We thereby are transformed in *who we are* and in *how we exist*, not just in what we believe. God has manifested faithfulness toward humans in covenant relationships and in giving us astonishing gifts. So we must be actively faithful toward God with all that we are and have. This is basic to genuine filial knowledge of God. Nothing requires that God supply our propositional knowledge that God exists apart from our filial knowledge of God. Ideally God promotes the two together.

We can now distinguish *theoretical theism* and *filial theism*. Theoretical theism affirms that God exists. It is often coupled with the view that some people *know*, or at least *reasonably believe*, that God exists. Theoretical theism, however, will not resolve our common human predicament. A key human deficiency regarding God is in our moral orientation regarding *lordship* over our lives. Insisting on our own lordship, we are alienated from God. In the interest of genuine personal reconciliation, God does not settle for our accepting theoretical theism. Our having a friendship requires more than our knowing that a friend exists. So God promotes our embracing *filial* theism. This is the view that we are properly children of the God who as our loving Father merits our respectfully and gratefully *believing in*, or trusting, God *as the Lord of our lives*. Theoretical theism is fine as far as it goes. It does not go far enough, however, for God's redemptive concerns. Filial theism goes beyond belief that God exists, in recommending a filial life-commitment to a personal Lord. God wants us to be members *living* in God's family, not just people who believe that God's family exists.

Filial knowing of God requires our knowing God as Lord *in the second-person*, as supreme "You." Lordship entails supreme moral leadership, and *moral leadership* entails a call to moral accountability and direction. When self-centered humans are the recipients, God's call is for moral redirection and transformation toward God's character of sacrificial love. Knowing God *as Lord* requires our surrendering to God as follows: "Not my will, but Your will," "Not my kingdom, but Your kingdom." Filial knowing of God thus points to Gethsemane and the cross of Jesus. It depends on our volitional sensitivity and submission to the will of God. Such knowing requires a genuine commitment to obey God's call, even if the call is to give up one's life in sacrificial love on a criminal's cross. We thus come truly to know God not in our prideful cognitive glory but rather in our volitional weakness relative to the priority of *God's* will. Such humble knowing is indispensable to Hebraic filial knowledge of God. Our willful pride must not get in the way of our embracing the God of *gracious* (rather than earned) love. As Jesus showed in Gethsemane, our will must take second place to God's loving will. Otherwise, filial knowledge is impossible.

A pressing issue is: are we *entitled* to know God? Do we humans have a right to know that God exists without knowing God *as Lord*, as the morally supreme agent for our lives? Some people uncritically assume an affirmative answer and thereby neglect filial knowledge of God. An even prior question is: *who* is entitled to decide how one may know God—we humans or God? Given our status relative to God, can *we* reasonably make demands on God, including demands about knowing God? Perhaps God's dispensing of knowledge of God is truly gracious, a genuine gift calling for grateful reception. Many people presume that we have a *right* to know God on our preferred terms. In virtue of what, however, does God owe us revelation and knowledge of God?

God's ways of imparting knowledge of God may differ significantly from our natural expectations regarding God. How we may know God depends perhaps on what God lovingly wants *for us* and *from us*. So as knowers we may be responsible *to God*, and not just to ourselves and our prior cognitive commitments. Perhaps, moreover, we can truly come to know God only if we acknowledge our unworthiness of knowing God. It may thus be illuminating to ask about the attitudes of people inquiring about God. What are our *intentions* in having knowledge of God? Do we have a bias against filial knowledge of God? Do we resist knowing God as personal Lord who lovingly holds us morally accountable and expects grateful obedience from us as God's children? Such crucial issues rarely emerge in discussions about knowledge of God, but they bear nonetheless on real human attitudes.

Philosopher Thomas Nagel has a "cosmic authority problem" with theism. In his words: "...I hope there is no God! I don't want there to be a God; I don't want the universe to be like that."[12] Nagel confesses to having a fear of any religion involving God. Such fear seems widespread among humans. It stems from human fear of losing human lordship over human decisions and life. Such self-protective fear resists God's liberating ways of unselfish love. This kind of fear prompted an atheist friend of mine to report that he would kill himself if he had to acknowledge God's reality. The sad attitudes of Nagel and my friend regarding God speak volumes about the human condition. Such attitudes self-destructively banish God from human lives.

ARE "SIGNS AND WONDERS" NEEDED FOR KNOWLEDGE OF GOD?

❧ Chapter 3 ❧

The Hebraic God is the God of miracles. How do miracles figure in knowledge of God? Shouldn't God be less stingy with miracles, including altogether amazing observable events? Hebraic theism disallows God's being trivialized as an object of amazement for our convenient examination or speculation. It calls for knowledge of God *as Lord* who is the supreme personal guide and gift-giver for human life. This God is the lovingly commanding agent to whom we are ultimately morally responsible. This is the final personal authority over all creation, including over human knowers. In filial knowledge of God, we have knowledge of a supreme *personal subject*, not of a mere *object* for casual reflection. This is not knowledge of a vague First Cause, Ultimate Power, Ground of Being, or even a Best Explanation. It is *convicting* knowledge of a personal, communicating Lord who demands full grateful commitment in response to God's gracious salvation. In love, God convicts us of our wayward tendencies. Such convicting knowledge includes our being judged, and found unworthy, by the standard of God's love.

God aims that all people freely choose to be transformed by God from self-serving to self-giving, loving children of the God of morally serious love. (For suggestions of this ideal, see Deuteronomy 6:5, 10:12-13; Leviticus 19:18; Mark 12:28-30; John 15:9-17). As all-loving, God desires that eventually all people freely come to be morally and lovingly perfect as God is morally and lovingly perfect (Matthew 5:48). Given this aim, God is not required to offer *undeniable*, or *insuppressible*, evidence that would produce universal *mere* propositional knowledge that God exists. Love of God, like ordinary friendship, cannot be coerced but must be freely given, and God is in the full-time business of promoting love of God. In respecting human freedom, God has offered evidence of God that allows for deniability of God's existence. God does not generally value knowledge that God exists apart from filial knowledge of God. For our own good, God desires that we know God *as God*, specifically, as *our gracious Father*. God is *cognitively sovereign* and *morally demanding*. God lovingly sets the conditions for approaching God, and the conditions set are sensitive to our moral attitude toward God. We have no firm basis to demand that God meet our own favored ways of approaching God.

REVELATION, SIGNS, AND WONDERS

The Hebraic approach to filial knowledge of God gives primacy to *revelation from God*. It thus offers a top-down rather than a bottom-up approach to the source of filial knowledge of God. This explains the absence of esoteric philosophical reasoning about God in the Jewish and Christian scriptures. Filial knowledge of God is available to every sincere seeker at God's appointed time. Still, its realization comes via—and not in advance of—an attitude of sincere willingness to love God with the kind of love characteristic of God. This fits well with the Christian message that God *is* love, that is, inherently loving (see 1 John 4:8,16; cf. 2 Corinthians 13:11). Our resisting God's characteristic kind of love, including love of enemies, is to reject *God*. Paul thus notes that if he understands all mysteries and all knowledge but lacks God's love, he is nothing (1 Corinthians 13:2).

Each person must individually seek filial knowledge of God, just as each person must form his or her own friendships. You cannot give me your filial knowledge of God. Nor can anyone else. On God's side of the relationship, only God can show you God in a way that constitutes reconciling and morally transforming filial knowledge of God. Other people cannot accomplish this on their own for you. Our needed turning to God moves us away from selfishness, ingratitude, and self-righteousness—the core of resisting God. Such repentance is necessarily personal. It cannot be done by proxy. It is not, however, cognitively arbitrary. All mature human persons have evidence from moral conscience that their self-righteousness and selfishness lack support from the quality of their actual moral character. Our frequently presumed status of superior moral importance is but misguided pride. We can know this on proper reflection. Our recurring moral pride is indeed a thin veneer, *perhaps* lightly covering but not genuinely improving who we really are.

Critics will object that God's presence is too ambiguous to merit reasonable acknowledgment. God owes us more miraculous signs and wonders, whatever God's redemptive aims. Why doesn't God convince us, once and for all, with decisive manifestations of God's awesome power? It would cost God nothing, and it would vanquish nagging doubts about God's existence. A truly loving God would use miraculous powers to free us from our doubts. God's redemptive purposes, many will thus object, do not exonerate God from the charge of excess restraint in manifestation. If God exists, God is blameworthy for inadequate self-revelation.

Philosopher Norwood Russell Hanson complains about the absence of observable happenings that establish God's existence. "There is no single natural happening, nor any constellation of such happenings, which establishes God's existence....If the heavens cracked open and [a] Zeus-like figure ... made his presence and nature known to the world, *that* would establish such a happening."[13] Hanson observes that nothing like the Zeus-event has ever occurred so as to recommend theism to all reasonable people. He thus concludes that theism lacks adequate warrant for universal acceptance.

Critics such as Hanson exhibit misguided expectations about what exactly astonishing signs will accomplish. Astonishing signs, like ordinary events, are interpretively flexible. They logically admit of various coherent interpretations, including nonmiraculous interpretations. Miraculous events do not impose their interpretations on us. We interpreters must decide on our interpretations of events, and various background beliefs and motives typically influence our interpretive decisions. We thus should not regard miraculous signs as effective *for all inquirers*. A miraculous sign can prompt and build trust toward God in people genuinely open to God's intervention, but not in all people. The best and correct explanation of a striking event may be that it is miraculous. Suppose, however that your background assumptions were thoroughly materialistic, acknowledging only physical entities as real. In that case, an explanation acknowledging miracle would not prevail for you by your standards. You would then find an alternative treatment of the striking event. Perhaps you would withhold judgment on its interpretation or appeal to illusion or even to extraterrestrial powers (e.g., UFO's).

Astonishing signs often fail to convince. People can minimize the force of such signs by making certain alterations in their beliefs. The New Testament suggests as much. "If [people] do not listen to Moses and the prophets, neither will they be convinced even if someone rises from the dead" (Luke 16:31). The Gospel of John concurs regarding the ineffectiveness of miraculous signs in producing faith. "After Jesus had said this, he departed and hid from them. Although he had performed so many signs in their presence, they did not believe in him" (John 12:36-37). Humans can reject even the loving signs from God's self-giving son.

If you demand a universally convincing undeniable manifestation of God, you should consider whether that is really a viable demand. For *any* amazing manifestation, you *could* coherently ascribe a source (however implausible) without making reference to God. The strange possibilities are endless; likewise for your wiggle room regarding God. Suppose, however, that you came to refer to God at a time. You would then persist in this reference only if you *trusted* God not to change in a way incompatible with the supreme title "God." Such personal trust exceeds one's apprehending an astonishing sign. God builds his kingdom on personal trust anchored in God's supreme love. This preserves the kind of personal freedom essential to genuine love.

Two Kinds of People and Signs

What about people open to God's intervention but not yet believing in God? Wouldn't they benefit from miraculous signs by coming to believe in God? Perhaps. Let's distinguish people *passively* open to belief in God and people *actively* open to belief in God. People passively open to such belief do not put any serious effort into examining whether God has intervened in history. Such people are "open" to God with striking indifference. This indifference manifests itself in failure to act in ways that take seriously the availability of evidence for God. Passive openness is mere lip service to taking a real interest in the availability of evidence for God. We do not appropriately *value* evidence for God if we lack a morally serious interest in the availability of such evidence. Passive openness is thus an improper, insufficiently serious attitude toward available evidence for God. It trivializes a matter of supreme importance.

People actively open to belief in God take a *morally serious* interest in the availability of evidence for God. Such an interest has potential morally transforming effects. These people are not morally indifferent about whether God has intervened in history. They take a morally serious interest in available evidence for God's intervention. People suitable for filial knowledge of God must be actively willing to be morally transformed toward the loving character of God. Are there such morally serious seekers who would believe in God if and only if they had firsthand a miraculous sign from God? This question suffers from vagueness in talk of a "miraculous sign" from God.

Let's distinguish *morally impotent* and *morally transforming* miraculous signs. Morally impotent miraculous signs can surprise and entertain people but cannot transform their moral character. Morally transforming signs, in contrast, change one's moral character toward the moral character of God. People often seek mere entertainment from visible phenomena. God, however, seeks our moral transformation from the inside out. For our own good, God is not in the entertainment business regarding our coming to know God. Isaiah 58:2 portrays God as complaining about the Israelites that "day after day they seek me and delight to know my ways, as if they were a nation that practiced righteousness and did not forsake the ordinance of their God." The New Testament likewise discourages our seeking after morally impotent signs from God. It promises, however, a morally transforming sign to genuine seekers after God. Since this sign is a definitive sign from the God of morally serious love, it manifests the character of God. It thus manifests God's morally serious love. The New Testament confirms this expectation, explicitly and repeatedly. (See 2 Corinthians 5:16-17; 1 John 4:12-13,16,19.) Paul thus remarks that hope in God does not disappoint us "because God's love has been poured out in our hearts" by God's Spirit (Romans 5:5).

The presence of God's morally transforming love is the key *cognitive* foundation for filial knowledge of God. Such divine love is a foundational source of knowledge of God (Colossians 2:2; 1 Corinthians 8:2-3; Ephesians 3:17-19.) It is real *evidence* of God's reality and presence. This love is a personal intervention by God and the basis of a personal relationship with God. It is the presence of a personal God. So the filial knowledge in question exceeds propositional knowledge. It rests on morally transforming love from God that produces a loving character in children of God, despite their obstruction at times. This transformation *happens to one*, in part, and thus is neither purely self-made nor simply the byproduct of a self-help strategy. This widely neglected supernatural sign is available at God's appointed time to anyone who turns to God with moral seriousness. It transforms one's will to yield gratitude, trust, and love toward God and love toward other people. So: "We know that we have passed from death to life because we love one another.... Whoever does not love does not know God, for God is love" (1 John 3:14, 4:8, NRSV). So we need to learn how to apprehend, and to be apprehended by, God's supreme *love* for all of us, not just *truths about* God's love. Neither God nor God's love is a proposition or an argument. Neither is reducible to an intellectual construct.

The evidence of God's presence offered by loving character-transformation in God's children is crucial. It goes much deeper than the comparatively superficial evidence found in entertaining signs, wonders, visions, ecstatic experiences, and fancy philosophical arguments. We could consistently dismiss any such sign, wonder, vision, ecstatic experience, or argument as illusory or indecisive, given certain alterations in our beliefs. In contrast, genuine character transformation toward God's all-inclusive love does not admit of easy dismissal. It bears directly on who one really is, the kind of person one actually is. Such transformation cuts too deeply against our natural tendencies toward selfishness to qualify as just a self-help gimmick. It thus offers a kind of firm evidence that resists quick dismissal. Critics of Hebraic theism have uniformly failed to undermine such crucial evidence for God. Typically they ignore it. It thus escapes their self-limiting cognitive nets.

Entertaining signs and wonders are optional and not mandatory for God. They are not suitably morally transforming in the way required by filial knowledge of God. In this regard, they are markedly inferior to the supernatural sign from the transforming presence of God's love. An all-loving God would make God's presence *available* to humans at God's appointed time. God's presence, however, need not exceed the presence of God's love or be available apart from morally serious inquiry. God's presence need not include miracles irrelevant to moral transformation toward God's character, even though God may use such miracles as attention-getters. An all-loving God can properly make confident knowledge of God's existence arise simultaneously with filial knowledge of God. So God is exonerated from the charge of irresponsibly neglecting entertaining signs, so long as God reveals God's presence to anyone suitably receptive. Hanson's use of the Zeus-example overlooks these considerations. It trivializes God's actual aim. As all-loving, God aims to bring unloving people to love God and others, even enemies. One could not have a more difficult, or a more important, task.

God does try at God's appointed time to draw everyone into the kingdom of God, but God does not extinguish our free will. Neither God nor anyone else can coerce genuine gratitude, trust, or love. Free choice is a prerequisite for loving relationships. Forced friendship is no friendship at all. In keeping with full moral goodness, God seeks loving relationships above all else. God seeks the freely chosen grateful union of our wills with God's morally serious loving will. Only then is an all-inclusive loving community possible. Being all-loving, God seeks such a God-centered community above all else (John 13:34-35, 15:12-17, 17:20-23). Given the signs of personal excellence left by God in ourselves and other areas of creation, we *should* seek after God and thereby come to know God in a filial manner. Some people, however, will neglect the responsibility of seeking after God. The demands of discipleship are too inconvenient for many of us, given our chosen priorities. (See the Parable of the Sower, in Mark 4:3-20, for Jesus' diagnosis of unbelief.) We thus refuse to be displaced from the center of our universe. Still, God challenges our self-destructive blinders that aim to disregard God's program of all-inclusive redemption. We cannot plausibly blame God, then, for the blinders we sometimes stubbornly choose to wear.

HOW DO WISDOM AND EXPLANATION FIGURE IN KNOWLEDGE OF GOD?

❧ **Chapter 4** ❧

As our wills yield to God's excellence, we open ourselves to a kind of transforming wisdom and supernatural power unavailable from worldly wisdom. We then encounter a divine Father able and willing to liberate us from our own destructive, even self-destructive, ways. Paul captures this point succinctly. "My speech and my proclamation were not with plausible words of wisdom, but with a demonstration of the Spirit and of power, so that your faith might rest not in human wisdom but in the power of God" (1 Corinthians 2:4-5; cf. 1 Thessalonians 1:5). Talk is cheap indeed, but God's power is priceless. The power of God's Spirit appears not with competitive, prideful, or otherwise self-serving behavior. It rather involves such unworldly fruit as self-giving love and service. Accordingly the cross of Jesus is the standard of God's power (1 Corinthians 1:18). Paul lists some supernatural fruit of God's Spirit: love, joy, peace, patience, kindness, generosity, faithfulness, gentleness, and self-control (Galatians 5:22-23; see 1 Corinthians 13:4-7 on God-inspired love). Such fruit is as rare as it is excellent and is no mere self-help product. It rather is the yield of God's supernatural transformative power. God is the original bearer of such fruit. So we should approach God and knowledge of God accordingly.

God's merciful wisdom has authority and power of a special kind. It is a saving authority and power that works from within to avoid coercion, to preserve freedom, and to liberate us from bondage to selfishness.

Jesus captured the idea by telling his disciples that the authority of God comes through service rather than through wielding control over people (Mark 10:42-45). So Jesus accepted scandalous death on a criminal's cross, thus manifesting God's self-giving, sacrificial love to the very end. God, through Jesus, reconciles us by manifesting self-giving love and by calling us to follow suit (cf. 2 Corinthians 5:19). The disturbing authority of Jesus is all about laying down our personal rights in love, for the sake of the good of others. It is thus the direct opposite of worldly authority. Indeed, it is foolishness in the world's eyes (cf. 1 Corinthians 1:22-29). Even so, the divine love involved in such authority is the anchor all humans need to avoid being swept away in fear, pride, and selfishness.

The love we receive from God is not only obligating (we have been purchased with a high price) but also empowering. It empowers us to live freely in God's self-giving love, thereby empowering others to do the same. Such empowering love is the God-given recipe for the building of God's everlasting kingdom. We sometimes fail to see the supernatural power in such love, because we tend not to value such love properly or we do not want its guidance in our lives. We thus miss the empowering self-revelation offered by God. At times we even presume to have the power of sacrificial love solely within ourselves. This, however, is an illusion of our pride. Our lives tell the real truth about us. We need God's empowering Spirit of love to live in love. True sacrificial love is "from God" (1 John 4:7). It is not ours to trumpet. Our boasting should thus be in God, not in ourselves.

We have touched on the relevance of wisdom to knowledge of God. What, however, is wisdom, and what does love have to do with wisdom? Aristotle, in the *Nicomachean Ethics* (1141a), portrays wisdom as the most finished of the forms of knowledge and links it with *excellence*. Wisdom in general is knowledge, or sound discernment, of what is excellent. What is excellent in a certain domain of existence is what is *the best available* in that domain. Wisdom regarding our own human kind is just sound discernment of what is excellent for human character and human intellectual and practical life. Wisdom thus exceeds knowledge. We can have knowledge of many things but lack sound discernment of what is excellent for human character and life. Our having justified true beliefs does not guarantee our having sound discernment of what is excellent for us. Many people have extensive knowledge while their lives remain in shambles. Many such people lack the perspective of genuine wisdom, of sound discernment of what is excellent for their lives.

WISDOM WITHOUT GOD?

The life of wisdom is just the life characterized by excellence. What qualifies as excellence for our lives depends on the kind of universe we inhabit, as it depends on the best *actually available* for our lives. A question of first importance is thus theological. Is there a god who loves us? Is there an all-loving being worthy of worship and full life-commitment? Most contemporary philosophers say no. This fits with a commitment to materialism, the view that all of reality is ultimately physical. The universe portrayed by materialism has no room for the all-loving Hebraic God, who is by nature non-material.

Bertrand Russell has vividly described the universe of materialism in his 1903 essay "A Free Man's Worship."

> Brief and powerless is Man's life; on him and all his race the slow, sure doom falls pitiless and dark. Blind to good and evil, ... omnipotent matter rolls on its relentless way. For Man, condemned today to lose his dearest, tomorrow himself to pass through the gate of darkness, it remains only to cherish ... the lofty thoughts that ennoble his little day; disdaining the coward terrors of the slave of Fate, to worship at the shrine that his own hands have built; undismayed by the empire of chance, to preserve a mind free from the wanton tyranny that rules his

outward life; proudly defiant of the irresistible forces that tolerate, for a moment, his knowledge ... despite the trampling march of unconscious power.[14]

Russell speaks of "blind" matter, thus suggesting that our universe has no lasting purpose or guide. Accordingly Russell refers to "the blind hurry of the universe from vanity to vanity" (p. 52).

Russell is explicit about our purposeless existence.

That Man is the product of causes which had no prevision of the end they were achieving; that his origin, his growth, his hopes and fears, his loves and his beliefs, are but the outcome of accidental collocations of atoms; ... that all the labours of the ages, all the devotion, all the inspiration, all the noonday brightness of human genius, are destined to extinction in the vast death of the solar system...—all these things, if not quite beyond dispute, are yet so nearly certain, that no philosophy which rejects them can hope to stand (p. 45).

So Russell proposes that we humans can proceed "only on the firm foundation of unyielding despair" (pp. 45-46). Russell's position of despair implies that Hebraic theism cannot hope to stand.

Russell portrays "wisdom" in terms of "the Stoic freedom" of submitting our desires to the reality of the hostile universe. Such submitting of desires requires that we not rebel with indignation against the universe. It requires that we resign ourselves to its hostility. Russell's brand of wisdom thus entails that "from the submission of our desires springs the virtue of resignation" (p. 49). So Russell's foundation of "unyielding despair" promotes resignation rather than indignation. Russell urges nonetheless that we help others suffering "in the same tragedy with ourselves," that we "instil faith [for others] in hours of despair" (p. 53). Russell does not say what we should instil faith *in*; nor is it clear that his materialism offers any real option for a worthwhile object of faith. Still, we should appreciate Russell's honesty about the ominous results of materialism, even though his confidence in materialism is overdrawn.

Russell acknowledges that his materialism leaves us with some "strange" and "inexhaustible" mysteries. We humans are one of the mysteries. "A strange mystery," according to Russell, "is that Nature, omnipotent but blind, ... has brought forth at last a child ... with the capacity of judging all the works of his unthinking Mother" (p. 46). Russell's materialism seems doomed to acknowledge mystery here, given its implication that we are "but the outcome of *accidental* collocations of atoms" (p. 45). Russell also speaks of the "inexhaustible mystery of existence" in general (p. 51). If the unconscious material world is just the result of accident, inexhaustible mystery is no surprise. Mere accident, whether in matter or in minds, has a way of being irredeemably mysterious.

In a 1936 essay, "Do We Survive Death?," Russell recommends his hypothesis of accident over any commitment to an intelligent designer of the universe. "The world in which we live can be understood as a result of muddle and accident; but if it is the outcome of deliberate purpose, the purpose must have been that of a fiend. For my part, I find accident a less painful and more plausible hypothesis."[15] Russell sketches a similar view in "A Free Man's Worship," proposing that the world's evil would make God evil if God existed. Two problems emerge, aside from Russell's oddly overlooking the role of free agents other than God in the origin of evil.[16] First, we should be wary of Russell's talk of the world's being *understood* as resulting from accident. The accident postulated by Russell leaves us with *unexplainable mystery* rather than understanding. Russell's postulating the accidental origin of our world does not yield an *explanation* of the world's origin. Rather, it disavows the availability of an explanation and thus of understanding. If the origin of the material world is truly accidental, it lacks the kind of components needed for explanation and understanding.

42

The second point concerns Russell's talk of the relative *plausibility* of his hypothesis of accident versus a thesis of intelligent design. By what standard is Russell's hypothesis of accident more plausible than Hebraic theism's commitment to a personal creator? Russell says that his hypothesis is "less painful" than theism. He would not argue, however, that the less painful of two hypotheses is more likely true. Perhaps a view about what kinds of things are *real* influences Russell's judgment of relative plausibility.

"Everything in the world is composed of 'events'," according to Russell, and "the notion of substance, in the sense of a permanent entity with changing states, is no longer applicable to the world."[17] Russell's view is puzzling. It seems that physical events, for example, are what physical *substances* undergo. It thus seems that events require substances. If a plausible hypothesis must accommodate Russell's view that there are only events and no permanent substances, Hebraic theism will automatically be implausible. The Hebraic God is no transitory event or series of such events. This God is an everlasting *agent*. So Russell's view of reality would preclude Hebraic theism. It would also account for his assertion of the relative *plausibility* of his hypothesis of accident.

Russell's general view of reality rests on his view that the natural sciences have cognitive priority over common sense and everything else. Russell acknowledges that the sciences begin with common-sense notions and judgments: notions of causation, space, time, things, etc. The sciences, however, often revise or eliminate such common notions to achieve their explanatory purposes. Russell observes that we typically start our theorizing from "naive realism," the view that things are just as they seem. We initially think that the objects we perceive really are as they appear. We think that snow is white, that fire is hot, that feathers are soft. The natural sciences, however, offer a strikingly different view. Our best physics entails that the features ascribed to external objects by naive realism do not really inhere in the external objects themselves. For example, our best physics entails that physical objects are devoid of color and gappy rather than continuous. Russell thus remarks that "naive realism leads to physics, and physics, if true, shows that naive realism is false."[18]

WISDOM AND ULTIMATE AUTHORITY

Should we follow Russell in taking the natural sciences as our ultimate cognitive authority? Russell holds that "the conscious purpose of philosophy ... ought to be solely to *understand* [or, to explain] the world as well as possible..."[19] Philosophy, in his view, should therefore seek the best available explanation of the world, including ourselves. This is indeed a major aim of philosophy, even if not the sole aim. Still, it is an open question whether the natural sciences have ultimate authority concerning the best available explanation of the world.

The view that the natural sciences *alone* have ultimate cognitive authority is *scientism*. Scientism is not itself a thesis of the natural sciences. Nor is it recommended by the natural sciences themselves. Scientism is a *philosophical* thesis about the authority of the sciences. So scientism is apparently self-defeating. It is not supported by its avowed sole source of ultimate cognitive authority—the natural sciences. The important point is that the natural sciences themselves do not conflict with Hebraic theism. Conflict arises when a theorist, going beyond the sciences, proposes that the natural sciences *alone* have ultimate cognitive authority. Such a theorist is then engaged in questionable, if not self-defeating, philosophy.

We now face a crucial question. How should we decide what merits ultimate authority for us regarding what we believe and do: for short, regarding our lives? Many people go through life without an *explicit* commitment to an ultimate authority for their lives. They still may have an implicit commitment to such an authority. The unexamined ultimate authority, however, is not worth having. It lacks the consistent guiding power it merits, at least relative to a person's commitments. Philosophy makes an important contribution when it identifies an ultimate authority for a person's life and clarifies its importance and viability.

What ultimate authority *should* we choose for our lives? How *should* we arrive at such a decision? Note the double occurrence of "should." Another question arises: should for what end? Without an answer to the latter question, we lack adequate understanding of what kind of requirement figures in our question of what ultimate authority we should adopt.

The end we select to delimit the sense of "should" will give definite sense to our question about what ultimate authority we should choose. It will also specify the ideal we value in our own decision-making. So it will manifest the kind of people we aim to be. Where our central ideals are, there also is our heart, the core of our personal character. Typically we adopt our ideals for decision-making in light of the ultimate ends we value. The natural sciences do not settle this matter for us. They do not recommend ultimate ends for us. The natural sciences proceed on the basis of certain ends valued by many scientists. The mind-independent world does not settle the present matter for us. It does not dictate our ultimate ends, even though it can preclude our satisfying certain ends. Our ultimate ends, for better or worse, are our own final responsibility.

If we aim for excellence in inquiry, we may specify our question clearly. Given the end, or ideal, of acquiring *truth that best accounts for the world*, including ourselves, what should our ultimate authority be? The answer is now straightforward. Aiming for excellence in inquiry, we should pursue true beliefs that contribute to the best available explanation of the world. We thus should acknowledge the existence of those things that figure in the best available explanation of the world. This is required by excellence in inquiry. If we aim for excellence in all available domains, we should acknowledge and pursue whatever makes for excellence in those domains, including the domains of belief, action, sentiment, and character. The kind of excellence a person acknowledges and pursues reveals the state of that person's character. Ideally we would seek excellence not just as *truth-seekers* but as *morally responsible agents as well.*

The Hebraic God plays a crucial role in the best available explanation of the world, including human moral agents. This God removes what Russell identified as the unexplainable mystery of the existence of a material world. A puzzling question merits attention. Why is there a material world rather than no such world at all? A second puzzling question arises. Why is there the present law-governed (perhaps statistical law-governed) material world rather than a world markedly different? The goal-directed intentions of the Hebraic God can supply an answer to such questions, thereby removing Russell's supposedly unexplainable mystery of the world's existence.[20]

The Hebraic God figures crucially in our best available explanation of (a) why there is a material world *rather than no such world at all* and (b) why there is the law-governed material world hospitable to the origin of human life *rather than a significantly different world*. God has causal powers that contribute to such explanation and thereby remove mystery. Even so, our seeing the things of God depends on God's "showing" them to us (Romans 1:19; 1 Corinthians 2:11-12; cf. 1 John 5:6-9,20). Cognitively, we need God to enable us to see the things of God. God's loving purposes account for the world's apparently being the kind of place designed to humble us and thereby to enable God to call us to God in our vital need (cf. Deuteronomy 8:1-3). God's existence does not remove all mystery for us. The existence of God, for instance, may always be a mystery to humans. We should not be surprised by this, however, given our extensive cognitive limitations.

Some relevant explanation-seeking questions concern ourselves as moral agents. Why are there such beings as ourselves with the remarkable feature of conscious free agency? We consciously act, for better or worse, on *intentions* to achieve our ends. We thus differ from the intellectually blind material world. The difference is not just that we can *think*. It includes our being able to act intentionally, with an end in view. We are purposive agents, able to act in a *goal-directed* manner. This is an astonishing fact about us, even if we often take it for granted. The Hebraic God's existence enables us to answer our question about free agents. God created beings in God's own image of conscious free agency to enable those beings to sustain loving relationships with God and with each other. We are dependent under-creators owing to our being created in the image of the original creator.

The Hebraic God is the perfect manifestation of personal excellence for free agents. So we may characterize wisdom for human agents in terms of knowing God in a filial manner. In virtue of knowing God, we come to know personal excellence for such free agents as ourselves. A truly excellent all-powerful God would give us an opportunity, without coercion, to achieve God's kind of moral excellence. God would enable us to be rescued, without coercion, from our moral deficiencies and thereby to become morally like God in filial relationship with God. Such an opportunity would be *volitional* and not just intellectual. It would enable us to have our *wills* transformed, not just our intellects. So the kind of knowledge of God constitutive of wisdom is volitionally transformative rather than merely intellectual. It entails self-sacrificing personal excellence that exceeds contemplation, insight, enlightenment, and ecstatic experience. Excellence in relationships among agents requires self-giving love and thus interpersonal trust. So any being worthy of the supreme title "God" must be in the full-time business of promoting such love and trust. God thus must be in the business of transforming such naturally unloving agents as ourselves into morally new people. We can now see, then, the important explanatory value of filial knowledge of the Hebraic God. It enables us to make good sense of our common human predicament.

HOW IS KNOWLEDGE OF GOD MADE SECURE?

℘ Chapter 5 ℘

FROM REFLECTION TO OBEDIENT LOVE

Our foundations for acknowledging the Hebraic God lead us beyond matters of explanatory power to moral transformation. A truly excellent God would be all-loving and therefore would work in human history to encourage free human agents to seek God's kind of moral excellence. In the absence of such saving work, God could still be *just*, or fair, if human agents have rebelled against God. God would not, however, be all-loving in that case. God would then be indifferent to rebellious humans in a way incompatible with self-giving love. When we look in human history for a self-giving God who manifests excellence, the history of ancient Israel sticks out like a sore thumb. It manifests patterns of human behavior and instruction best explained by the Hebraic view that God has chosen a people for God in order to transform, morally and spiritually, all the nations of the world (see Genesis 12:1-3, 26:4, 28:13-14; Acts 3:25; Galatians 3:8; Romans 4:16-18). These patterns of Hebraic history call out for explanation. They underwrite the Hebraic view that a God of personal excellence and powerful love has indeed tried to save humans from their self-destructive ways.

We do well to consider the importance of the biblical record of God's interventions in human history. This record is crowned by the messianic biography of the four Christian Gospels: the evangelistic biography of Jesus. In Jesus we find a kind of authoritative teaching and conduct that leaves us with the clear choice already noted. Either (a) he was patently insane, (b) he was demonic, or (c) he was the unique person he claimed to be, the unique son of God. We do well to pay serious attention to these stark options. Only one of them is sustainable given our evidence concerning Jesus.

Anyone genuinely open to excellence for us humans, including moral excellence, will see that Jesus was by no means insane or demonic. He was a living paradigm of sanity and even unsurpassed wisdom and goodness. He was exactly what one would expect, on proper reflection, of the human manifestation of a truly excellent God of self-giving love. Just as God is the perfect personal manifestation of wisdom, Jesus is the perfect human manifestation of wisdom. Jesus spoke of himself as the representative of God's wisdom (Luke 7:31-35; cf. Matthew 11:16-19). So if we acknowledge the authority of Jesus, the fact that Jesus was fully committed to God as a loving father offers us a compelling reason to follow suit. Jesus as Lord should be our life-model for relating to his Father and our Father (Matthew 10:24-25; John 13:13-17; 1 Corinthians 11:1).

Our calling on God as our Father will properly lead to the kind of repentance and filial knowledge preached by Jesus. God's self-revelation of transforming love will thereby take us beyond mere historical and scientific probabilities to a secure foundation of *personal acquaintance* with God. As Paul remarks, in our sincerely crying out "Abba, Father" to God (note the Jesus-inspired filial content of this cry), God's Spirit confirms to our spirit that we are indeed children of God (Romans 8:16; cf. Romans 10:6-9; Deuteronomy 30:14; John 10:16,27; 1 John 5:6-9). We thereby receive God's personal assurance of our filial relationship with God. This assurance is more robust than any kind of theoretical certainty offered by philosophers or theologians. It liberates us from dependence merely on the quagmire of speculation, hypothesis-formation, or probabilistic inference about God. Such assurance yields a distinctive kind of grounded firm confidence in God unavailable elsewhere. *God* thus merits credit even for proper human confidence in God (Ephesians 2:8). So humans who boast of their own intellectual resources in knowing

God have misplaced boasting. God as Gift-Giver offers the confidence we cannot muster on our own, however shrewd we are.

Russell has objected to the Christian view of repentance, in his influential essay "Why I Am Not a Christian." "When you hear people in church debasing themselves and saying that they are miserable sinners, ... it seems contemptible and not worthy of self-respecting beings. We ought to stand up and look the world frankly in the face."[21] Hebraic theism recommends, in contrast, that we first look *ourselves* in the face. We may very well have a plank blinding our eyes from seeing our own moral condition, including our self-righteous pride. Whether we are what Russell calls "miserable sinners" may depend on what God, as the personification of moral excellence, demands of us. Judging ourselves by the moral standard exemplified in the life and teaching of Jesus, many of us must confess that we have failed miserably. I, for one, have never met a person who claims to have always loved God with all his heart, soul, mind, and strength and to have always loved his neighbor as himself. Given this standard, even Russell would have to confess miserable failure. To the extent that we violate the standard set by Jesus, we are slaves to selfishness and we need to be set free. The wisdom of the world lacks the power needed to free us. Our fears of personal loss and death, and our self-centered ways resulting from those fears, die hard indeed. It is thus no surprise that "Fear not" is one of the most common biblical injunctions.

Russell's moral standard evidently implies that he is not a "miserable sinner." Otherwise, Russell would have no basis for rejecting the Christian view that we are sinners needing transformation. Whatever alternative moral standard one offers, we must ask whether it demands something less than personal excellence from humans. The key issue will be whether the kind of self-giving love demanded and exemplified by Jesus is required for personal excellence. This issue brings us to our ultimate values, values that do not depend on any deeper values. Our ultimate values constitute who we really are and guide how we exist as persons. God's transforming values based on self-giving love make us new people via our filial relationship with God. (On the newness that God promises and brings, see Jeremiah 31:27-34, 32:37-40; Ezekiel 36:26; John 3:3-8; 2 Corinthians 5:14-19; 1 Peter 1:22-23.)

Proper seeking after God goes beyond mere reflection to eventual loving submission to God as the personal authority over all things. The big risk is that we have to relinquish our own idols, our own selfish priorities. Many people choose not to take this risk at all. Jesus made it clear that the good news he preached was also *difficult* news, news that requires full renunciation of old, self-centered ways of living (cf. Mark 10:17-27; Luke 14:25-35). So Jesus concluded his Sermon on the Mount with the sad news that few people actually find the gate leading to life (Matthew 7:13-14). We certainly will overlook the life-giving gate if we share Russell's suggestion that we are not failures on our own. In that case, we will not see our desperate need of the God who alone can give life.

Wisdom is the discernment of excellence, and God is the perfect manifestation of personal excellence. So the pursuit of wisdom requires pursuit of filial knowledge of God, including God's self-giving love. Jesus taught and lived God's lesson of self-giving love impeccably and thus is the very heart of God's wisdom. We need to value, then, not only the love of wisdom but also the self-giving love, in Jesus, definitive of God's wisdom. We also need to acknowledge that the authority of personal excellence, exemplified by God in Jesus, invites and then waits to be invited rather than coerces. God so loved the world that God gave us Jesus. God does not coerce us to receive the unmatched gift of self-giving love. God rather sends Jesus to knock, in sacrificial love, at the door of our heart in the hope that we will be hospitable (Revelation 3:20). Impartial reason, if there is such a thing, cannot test this kind of superhuman loving authority. God aims for the willing transformation of all reasoners to become children of God living by the power of God's own loving excellence.

Our response to God's program will define the kind of people we are: self-giving or self-serving. It will also determine whether we can plausibly regard our lives as having lasting value rather than the futility and despair of materialism acknowledged by Russell. If our lives lack enduring value, they have no robust, lasting meaning and thus invite despair, at least for the long term. Materialists, following Russell, may hold out for *short-lived* meaning. Even so, only a life with *enduring* value can stave off the unyielding despair that threatens any reflective life without God. The Hebraic God guarantees that lives united volitionally with God in excellence will survive the destruction of death through personal resurrection and thereby have lasting value. Fortunately, we thereby have a more excellent alternative than Russell's avowed despair. This troubled world has a silver lining after all.

The Christian alternative to despair is not just a hope for the future. It is realized in part *now*. God's wisdom is realized now when we are united with Christ in faithful filial obedience to God. We thereby witness to the reality of God's personal excellence. Christian faith is thus no merely intellectual matter of assenting to propositions. It is rather our trusting in God whereby we yield and conform to the gracious will of God. Such faith requires our being united volitionally with Jesus, the very image of God the Father. So Paul spoke of *the obedience of faith* (Romans 1:5, 16:26; cf. Romans 10:16; Acts 6:7; 1 Peter 1:21-22). The wise person, then, is the faithful filial witness to God's loving excellence. Wisdom without God leaves us at best with the hopeless despair of Russell. Wisdom with God leaves us with the empowered loving excellence of Jesus. Our decision between the two may seem easy but is actually demanding and ongoing. On either life-forming option, we all must count the high cost every day of our lives (Luke 9:23). We should handle a commitment against despair and for God with due humility and love at all times. Our aim will then be to reflect the One who personifies humility and love. Let's turn finally to the real cost of following Jesus in filial relationship with his Father.

We must not leave talk of God's gracious love and excellence abstract and impractical. Paul gives such talk an immediately practical value. He states that God's salvation is "through our Lord Jesus Christ, who died for us *in order that* ... we may live with him" (1 Thessalonians 5:10). The practical value of God's gracious redemption is that we may "live with" him and his reconciling son. God thus wants to "live with" people. Indeed, this is the remarkable story line of the whole Bible. Live with people *how?* Paul answers clearly. "For the following reason Christ died and lived again: *in order that* he might exercise lordship over the dead and the living" (Romans 14:9). Christ "died for all, *in order that* those who live might live no longer for themselves but for the one who died and was raised" (2 Corinthians 5:15). Having been purchased with a matchless price of sacrificial love at God's expense, we are no longer our own. We are to live in service to God and God's kingdom rather than to ourselves (1 Corinthians 6:19-20, 7:22-23). So God's merciful reconciliation aims for our living in community with God under the lordship of God's reconciling son. Community under any other lordship is pseudo-community.

Genuine lasting community requires unselfish love among its members. Human love is untainted by fear and resulting selfishness only as it is supplied and mediated by the Hebraic God. This God is our only empowering source of unselfish love. We must draw from God's empowering source of unselfish love by allowing the good news of God's gracious reconciliation to saturate our minds, wills, and emotions. In gratitude, we must then allow it to spill over into all our attitudes and actions toward others. Appropriation of God's gracious love in our individual lives thus empowers and sustains the kind of unselfish love required for genuine lasting community.

Our relying on God's gracious love is of *chief* importance. This explains Jesus' otherwise puzzling hyperbolic remark that whoever comes to him without "hating" immediate relatives and even life itself cannot be his disciple (Luke 14:26; cf. Matthew 10:37). It also explains Paul's striking remark that he was determined to know nothing among the Corinthians except Jesus Christ and him crucified (1 Corinthians 2:2). The crucifixion of Jesus, God's innocent son, is the pinnacle of God's self-giving love toward us. God so loved us all that Jesus came from God to die for us. Paul agrees. "God demonstrates his own love toward us, in that while we were yet sinners, Christ died for us" (Romans 5:8, NASB; cf. 1 John 4:9).

The reconciling death and resurrection of Jesus empower genuine community by freeing us from bondage to our fear, selfishness, self-righteousness, and our accompanying guilt and shame. We no longer have need of the latter burdens given what God has accomplished for us through Jesus. We can now risk living for God and others in resurrection joy. God sustained and vindicated Jesus by resurrection to imperishable life. Likewise God will sustain and vindicate people faithfully following Jesus in self-giving commitment. So for the sake of lasting community, God's gracious reconciliation seeks renunciation of our selfish autonomy, our exercising lordship in place of God. We must die to our self-crediting ways in order to live to God, specifically to Jesus' ways of self-giving love and community. We must be crucified with Christ (Galatians 2:19-20; cf. Colossians 3:1-4).

Our death to selfish autonomy is no loss of value at all. Such autonomy is not genuine freedom, but is rather slavery to fearful insecurity, self-seeking ambition, and an illusion of ultimate self-control. We are too fearful and weak to love as God loves. Loyalty to the self-giving Christ, in contrast, brings liberation from bondage and final death (Romans 6:15-23; John 8:34-36). Through God's Spirit dispatched by Jesus, we are to become fully loving grace-givers in the manner of God. God's grace is the glue needed to unite members of any lasting community.

Our being Spirit-led citizens of God's new, liberated creation requires the death of our old, selfish tendencies (Ephesians 4:20-24). The Christian calling is thus a call to suffer and to die with Christ (Galatians 2:19-21; Philippians 3:7-11; Romans 6:3-14; Colossians 2:11-12). Jesus puts the idea starkly. Whoever does not follow him by carrying the cross of suffering, self-giving love cannot be his disciple (Matthew 10:38-39; cf. Mark 8:34-35). After Jesus made such remarks, according to John's Gospel (6:53-66), many of his disciples complained that this teaching is too difficult and then stopped following him. True grace is thus unsettling and even divisive (Matthew 10:34-36; Mark 3:31-35; 1 Corinthians 11:18-19), owing to selfish resistance in its audience. The Christian calling nonetheless is inherently cross-shaped, after the pattern of Jesus. If we are not dead serious about this calling, we should not answer it at all (Luke 14:28-33). Jesus' death purchased no part-time disciples; nor is it just a *substitute* for us. Christians are to be full-time *imitators* of the self-giving life and death of Jesus (1 Corinthians 11:1; Philippians 2:5-13; cf. Leviticus 19:2). Jesus suffered out of love for others, and his followers must do likewise.

God works redemption, or reconciliation, in us through the weakness of suffering and death, in order to demonstrate that genuine saving power is altogether God's (1 Corinthians 1:17-25; 2 Corinthians 4:7-11, 12:8-10). God demonstrates through God's power in our weakness that no human has a right to boast in God's presence (1 Corinthians 1:29). Our own strengths, real or apparent, do not amount to the saving power belonging to God alone. Trust and hope based on the power of humans, rather than on the power of God, are as redemptively impotent as humans themselves. Indeed, God's grace supplemented by human credit cancels grace. All spiritual power comes to us on God's Christlike terms of human weakness rather than on our self-promoting terms. So our boast and hope should be in God alone (1 Corinthians 1:31; cf. 2 Corinthians 13:4). God's redemptive power is set in sharp relief against a background of human weakness. Anyone contradicting this lesson with a triumphalist self-exalting attitude betrays God's good news by offering a self-serving counterfeit corrupted by human power (2 Corinthians 11:1-12, 12:1-10). Any such person is, by Paul's lights, an "enemy of the cross of Christ" (Philippians 3:18). Intellectual triumphalism is especially threatening to those of us accustomed to much reflection.

Paul identifies the goal of suffering the loss of all things for Christ as mandatory for Christian discipleship, even for "knowing Christ" (Philippians 3:7-11). Paul notes, in Philippians 2:7-8, that Jesus himself set the model for discipleship by suffering the loss of all things in self-emptying obedience to God. According to Philippians 3, we should follow the model of Jesus. Paul's discipleship goal is "to know Christ and the power of his resurrection and the fellowship of his sufferings, being conformed to his death, if somehow I may arrive at the resurrection of the dead" (Philippians 3:10-11). This kind of knowing Christ is an intimate, loving, and transforming *personal relationship*. It is thus no mere intellectual matter. It is full self-commitment to a personal agent, not just to ideas or principles.

Why does Paul link knowing Christ with suffering the loss of all other things? The answer comes from Paul's talk of the necessity of regarding all other things as trash, or excrement, in order to gain Christ (Philippians 3:8). We must genuinely deem all other things as worthless "because of the surpassing value of personal knowledge of Christ Jesus my Lord" (3:8). Personal knowledge of Christ, the Lord of the universe, is of incomparable value relative to all other things. We thus must treasure such knowledge, such relationship, above all else. So we shall be in a position to receive the gift of such knowledge only if we put all other things in relative perspective. They are at best garbage in comparison. In the tradition of Jesus' demanding portrayal of discipleship, Paul's theme is difficult indeed. Even so, we are not dealing with ordinary knowledge. We are considering personal knowledge of God and God's unique son. Such knowledge requires complete honor and gratitude toward its exalted personal object (Romans 1:21). We must know God and his unique son *as God, as exalted, incomparable Lord of all things*. Otherwise, personal knowledge of God is unavailable. This, we noted, is for our own good. God will not compromise the unsurpassed value of one's knowing God.

Paul suggests that Christian suffering yields hope of a kind that does not disappoint us (Romans 5:3-5). Suffering with Christ produces a special kind of hope for God's deliverance. This is hope that God himself shores up with his loving presence. Blessed are those who suffer with Christ, then, for God's purifying gracious presence will fortify and comfort their hopeful hearts (cf. Matthew 5:4,8). This leads Paul to recommend that we should boast, even rejoice, in our sufferings (2 Corinthians 7:4, 12:9-10; Colossians 1:24). Sufferings can reveal God's distinctive powerful presence and thereby further God's redemptive work. By God's Spirit, our sufferings empty us of our self-exalting tendencies and our supposed self-sufficiency. They thus enable us to be filled with God's self-giving grace via deeper trust in God (Romans 8:14-17). Our sufferings thereby become a basis for our rejoicing. They signify a coming time when God will wipe away every tear, and death and suffering shall be no more (Revelation 21:4).

We should think of the suffering Jesus as a life-model rather than a mere *substitute* for us. Jesus offered himself as a life-model (Luke 9:23-24, 4:27-33). Paul likewise offered Jesus as a life-model for Christians (Philippians 2:5-13, 3:7-11; Romans 8:17; cf. 1 Peter 2:20-25). In humbling himself, even to the point of suffering and death, Jesus showed us what our humble and all-compassionate God is really like and what *we* too should be like. Jesus showed us what it is to be truly a human person, a person fully in the image of God. To the extent that Jesus is actually our life-model, we too can be persons realizing the image and filial knowledge of God. We are to be persons reflecting, and thus witnessing to, the very glory of God (2 Corinthians 3:18). Our lives are to *show* that God is definitely real, in ways that add real *power* to our words. We are to be *living symbols* of our divine

Father. We must thus look two ways: back to what God has uniquely and lovingly done in Jesus and forward to what God will similarly do through us, after the life-pattern of Jesus.

We now see that proper knowledge of God is anything but ordinary. This is not surprising. Such knowledge concerns the most important personal subject in all of reality. This personal subject merits top priority in all areas of our lives. So proper knowledge of God must not be put on a par with our ordinary knowledge or otherwise trivialized. We must renounce whatever challenges its priority in our lives. Our knowledge of God will either be our top priority or it will fail to be realized. (Jesus said the same about discipleship.) God thereby upholds the supreme value of our knowing God, for our own good. The main point of our knowing God is that we, in filial relationship with God, become loving as God is loving. This news sounds difficult, but we are not on our own. God's transforming power of love will change us and will thereby show us that this is the best news imaginable for us. God's good news is unsurpassably good, because God is likewise good. We thus may confidently trust God with all that we are and all that we have. This is good news indeed, news worthy of our full life-commitment to God.

CONCLUSION

Why, then, isn't God more obvious? The question suffers from a misplaced emphasis. It should be redirected. Why do *we* fail to apprehend God's loving reality and presence? Recall our opening statement of Russell's reply to God: "God, you gave us insufficient evidence." In God's presence, we do well to question *ourselves* rather than to blame God. Russell overlooked this lesson, as we all do at times. In our willful pride, we often overlook God's supreme ways of humble love. If our hearts are willingly attuned to God's self-giving transformative love, God will be obvious enough. We thus need proper eyes to see and ears to hear the reality of God. To that end, we need to call on the Lord, who *alone* can empower our appropriation of the things of God. The Hebraic God of love will then answer in love. All things will then become new, under God's powerful transforming love. So "taste and see that the Lord is good" (Psalm 34:8).[22]

ENDNOTES

[1] E.P. Sanders, *The Historical Figure of Jesus* (London: Penguin, 1993), pp. 168, 242. Similarly, see Graham Stanton, *Gospel Truth?* (Valley Forge, Penn.: Trinity Press International, 1995), pp. 173-87.

[2] E.P. Sanders, "The Life of Jesus," in Hershel Shanks, ed., *Christianity and Rabbinic Judaism* (Washington, D.C.: Biblical Archaeology Society, 1992), p. 78. For helpful discussion of the reliability of the New Testament materials about Jesus, see F.F. Bruce, *The New Testament Documents: Are They Reliable?*, 6th ed. (Grand Rapids: Eerdmans, 1981), and Craig Blomberg, *The Historical Reliability of the Gospels* (Downers Grove, Ill.: Intervarsity, 1987).

[3] James Dunn, *Jesus and the Spirit* (London: SCM, 1975), p. 38. For detailed treatment of this theme, see Bernard Cooke, *God's Beloved: Jesus' Experience of the Transcendent* (Philadelphia: Trinity Press International, 1992), pp. 1-24, 103-9. For evidence of a bias against God as Father in some influential atheists, see Paul Vitz, *Faith of the Fatherless* (Dallas: Spence, 1999).

[4] C.H. Dodd, *The Interpretation of the Fourth Gospel* (Cambridge: Cambridge University Press, 1953), p. 152. Likewise, see E.D. Schmitz, "Knowledge," in Colin Brown, ed., *New International Dictionary of New Testament Theology* (Grand Rapids: Zondervan, 1976), vol. 2, p. 396.

[5] G.J. Botterweck, *"Yada,"* in G.J. Botterweck and H. Ringgren, eds., *Theological Dictionary of the Old Testament*, revised ed. (Grand Rapids: Eerdmans, 1980), vol. 5, p. 469.

[6] Bernhard Anderson, *The Eighth Century Prophets* (Philadelphia: Fortress, 1978), pp. 56-57. See also Anderson, *Understanding the Old Testament*, abridged 4th ed. (Upper Saddle River, N.J.: Prentice Hall, 1999), pp. 278-79. For support Anderson cites Hosea 6:6 and Jeremiah 22:15-16.

[7] See the lucid discussion of this theme in Luke Timothy Johnson, *Living Jesus* (San Francisco: HarperCollins, 1999) and *The Real Jesus* (San Francisco: HarperCollins, 1996), pp. 153-66.

[8] Blaise Pascal, *Pensées*, revised ed., trans. A.J. Krailsheimer (London: Penguin, 1995). For discussion of Pascal's position, see Thomas V. Morris, *Making Sense of It All* (Grand Rapids: Eerdmans, 1992).

[9] On some species of idolatry, see Luke Timothy Johnson, *Faith's Freedom* (Minneapolis: Fortress, 1990), chapter 4, and *Sharing Possessions* (Philadelphia: Fortress, 1981), pp. 43-78.

[10] C.H. Dodd, *The Meaning of Paul for Today* (New York: Meridian, 1920), p. 131. Cf. Dodd's book on Jesus, *The Founder of Christianity* (London: Macmillan, 1970), pp. 51-52.

[11] For helpful reflections on the priority of God's love, see David F. Ford, *The Shape of Living* (Grand Rapids: Baker, 1998), pp. 55-71, 192-98; Leon Morris, *Testaments of Love* (Grand Rapids: Eerdmans, 1981), especially chapter 7; and Timothy P. Jackson, *Love Disconsoled* (Cambridge: Cambridge University Press, 1999). George MacDonald has captured God's effort to give love, as follows: "God finds it hard to give, because he would give the best, and man will not take it." See "Life," in MacDonald, *Unspoken Sermons*, Series 1-3 (Whitethorn, Cal.: Johannesen, 1997), p. 300.

[12] Thomas Nagel, *The Last Word* (New York: Oxford University Press, 1997), p. 130. Martin Heidegger may have had a similar cosmic authority problem. Richard Rorty classifies him with "people who are unable to stand the thought that they are not their own creations." See Rorty, *Contingency, Irony, and Solidarity* (Cambridge: Cambridge University Press, 1989), p. 109. Similarly, a friend's young daughter recently complained: "I don't like God. I didn't want him to make me. I wanted to make myself." For a candid autobiographical statement of volitional resistance to Christian commitment, see Mortimer Adler, *Philosopher at Large* (New York: Macmillan, 1977), pp. 315-16.

[13] Norwood Russell Hanson, *What I Do Not Believe and Other Essays* (Dordrecht: Reidel, 1971), p. 322.

[14] Bertrand Russell, "A Free Man's Worship," in *Mysticism and Logic* (Garden City, N.Y.: Doubleday, 1957), p. 54.

[15] Bertrand Russell, "Do We Survive Death," in *Why I Am Not a Christian* (London: Allen and Unwin, 1957), p. 93.

[16] On the role of free will in evil, including its significance in exonerating God, see Alvin Plantinga, *God, Freedom, and Evil* (New York: Harper & Row, 1974), and Daniel Howard-Snyder, ed., *The Evidential Argument from Evil* (Bloomington: Indiana University Press, 1996).

[17] Bertrand Russell, *Philosophy* (London: Allen and Unwin, 1927), pp. 287, 309.

[18] Bertrand Russell, *Inquiry into Meaning and Truth* (London: Allen and Unwin, 1940), p. 15.

[19] Russell, *Philosophy*, p. 310.

[20] On such why-questions, and their relation to the sciences, see Diogenes Allen, *Christian Belief in a Postmodern World* (Louisville: Westminster, 1989), especially Part I. Such questions also receive attention in Kenneth Miller, *Finding Darwin's God* (New York: HarperCollins, 1999).

[21] Bertrand Russell, "Why I Am Not a Christian," in *Why I Am Not a Christian*, p. 23.

[22] Many thanks to Paul Copan and Peter Bergeron for very helpful suggestions.

PROJECTED BOOKLETS IN THE RZIM
CRITICAL QUESTIONS SERIES

William Craig, *God, Are You There? Five Reasons God Exists and Three Reasons It Makes a Difference* (available)

Paul Copan, *Is Everything Really Relative? Examining the Assumptions of Relativism and the Culture of Truth Decay* (available)

Scott Armstrong, *Who's Shaping My Life? Assessing the Media's Influence on Our Culture*

Darrell Bock, *Can I Trust the Bible? Defending the Bible's Reliability* (available January 2001)

David K. Clark and James Beilby, *Why Bother With Truth? Arriving at Knowledge in a Skeptical Society* (available)

Douglas Geivett, *Can a Good God Allow Evil? Making Sense of Suffering*

Klaus Issler, *What Does It Mean To Be Human? Understanding Who We Really Are*

Mark Linville, *Is Everything Permitted? Moral Values in a World without God* (available January 2001)

L. T. Jeyachandran *Does the East Have the Answers? Getting Perspective on Eastern Religion and Philosophy*

Stuart McAllister, *Born to Shop? Exposing the Threat of a Consumer Culture*

Paul K. Moser, *Why Doesn't God Make Himself More Obvious? Understanding the God Who Hides and Seeks 9* (available)

Michael Ramsden, *What's the Point? Finding Meaning and Hope in God*

John Mark Reynolds, *Do the Bible and Science Conflict? Reconciling the Differences*

Ravi Zacharias, *What's So Special About Jesus? Encountering Christ Among the World's Religions*

Keith Pavlischek, *Should God Be Excluded from the Public Square? Undestanding the Role of Faith in the Public Life*

Charles Taliaferro, *Do Texts Have Any Meaning? Recovering Meaning and Truth in Texts*

Paul Chamberlain, *Whose Life is it Anyway? Assessing Physician-Assisted Suicide*

Christopher Wright, *Isn't the God of the Bible Cruel and Vindictive? Understanding Ethical Issues in the Bible*

William Lane Craig, *What Does God Know? Reconciling Divine Foreknowledge and Human Freedom*

Douglas Groothuis, *Lost in Cyberspace? Examining and Overcoming the Dehumanizing Effects of the Computer*

Sam Solomon, *Is Islam the One True Religion? Understanding and Engaging the Muslim Mind.*

If you have further questions or are in need of additional resources, please contact

Ravi Zacharias International Ministries,
4725 Peachtree Corners Circle, Suite 250,
Norcross, Georgia, USA 30092.

Website: **www.rzim.org**
Phone: **800.448.6766**
Fax: **770.729.1729**
E-mail: **rzim@rzim.org**

Regional Offices

Canada office
2476 Argentia Road ◆ Suite 203 Mississauga,
Ontario L5N 6M1 Canada ◆ 905.858.2980

European office
97A St. Aldate's,
Oxford OX1 1BT ◆ United Kingdom ◆ 44.1865.203.951

India office
P.O. Box 7307 ◆ Anna Nagar West Extension,
Chennai 600 101 ◆ India ◆ 91.44.626.8014

RZIM is a ministry founded by Dr. Ravi Zacharias with the goal to reach and challenge those who shape the ideas of a culture with the credibility of the message of Jesus Christ.

◦━━◦

If you are interested in obtaining a first-rate philosophical journal written with articles written by leading Christian philosophers, we encourage you to subscribe to *Philosophia Christi*, the journal of the Evangelical Philosophical Society (EPS). Please contact:

Paul Pardi
35706 25th Pl. South
Federal Way, WA 98003
eps8451@epsociety.org

◦━━◦

Published by RZIM
Ravi Zacharias International Ministries
4725 Peachtree Corners Circle, Suite 250
Norcross, Georgia 30092
www.rzim.org

───────────────────────

Library of Congress Cataloging-in-Publication Data
Moser, Paul, 2000
Why Isn't God More Obvious?
ISBN 1-930107-16-1

1. Knowledge, Theory of (Religion).
2. Christianity-Philosophy.